LIBRARY GAMES ACTIVITIES KIT

Ready-to-Use Activities for Teaching Library Skills in 20 Minutes a Week

PATTI HULET

**THE CENTER FOR APPLIED
RESEARCH IN EDUCATION**
West Nyack, New York 10995

Library of Congress Cataloging-in-Publication Data

Hulet, Patti, 1950
    Library games activities kit : ready-to-use activities for
teaching library skills in 20 minutes a week / Patti Hulet.
        p. cm.
    Includes indexes.
    ISBN 0-87628-543-4
    1. Elementary school libraries—Activity programs. 2. School
children—Library orientation. 3. Educational games. I. Center
for Applied Research in Education. II. Title.
Z675.S3H75 1990
0.25.5′68′222—dc20   90-2355
                                                                          CIP

ISBN 0-87628-543-4

THE CENTER FOR APPLIED
RESEARCH IN EDUCATION
BUSINESS & PROFESSIONAL DIVISION
A division of Simon & Schuster
West Nyack, New York 10995

Printed in the United States of America

To the students and staff at MacArthur School—
my family for so many years!

ABOUT THE AUTHOR

Patti Hulet taught for thirteen years in the Mesa Public Schools, Mesa, Arizona, as an elementary school media specialist. She now works as an educational consultant and manages Bookwings, a book service for selling children's books. She earned her BS in Education at the University of Idaho, her Arizona K–12 library endorsement at the University of Arizona, and her MS in Audiovisual Education at Arizona State University.

ACKNOWLEDGMENTS

Material in "That's a Fact!" and "Let Your Knowledge Blossom" first appeared as "That's a Fact!" *The School Librarian's Workshop,* April, 1987, pp. 5–6.

"Ocean of Words" first appeared as "Focus on the Thesaurus," *School Library Media Activities Monthly,* January, 1988, pp. 34–37, 44.

"Reference Race" first appeared as "Reference Race," *The School Librarian's Workshop,* April, 1988, pp. 3–4.

"Design Magic" first appeared as "Designing Coordinates," *The School Librarian's Workshop,* January, 1989, p. 9.

Pages from the *1888–1988 National Geographic Centennial Index* used by kind permission of the National Geographic Society.

ABOUT THIS RESOURCE

Did you know that beavers have orange teeth? That all eight legs of a spider are attached to its head? I learned these and many other interesting facts while working with first graders on our first research project together in "That's a Fact!" While some may say that first grade is too early to start teaching research skills, our learning experience began the moment the children first entered the library media center.

As classroom teachers and library media specialists, our goal is for the students to become independent learners, able to find needed information on their own. We want children to love to come to the library media center and to find that learning about *any* subject can be fun and exciting. We want students to develop good research habits from the start, not to have to deal with frustrations. Students need to feel confident that they can do research independently and enjoy it, because it is a skill they will use throughout their lives.

Library Games Activities Kit is a culmination of my efforts during thirteen years as an elementary school library media specialist to establish a fun, effective program for teaching library and research skills to kindergarten through sixth grade. The forty-five games and activities in this book are divided into three main sections:

1. Getting to know the Library Media Center—learning where to find everything
2. Using Reference Sources—picking the best source and getting the needed information
3. Understanding the Research Process—analyzing what to do

The appendix includes a merit award system and alphabetical, grade-level, subject, and activity-type indexes

Time is short—there is so much to be taught today! Therefore, the *Library Games Activities Kit:*

- breaks down big skills into smaller steps that can be sequentially taught over the years at the appropriate grade levels
- focuses on specific skills one at a time in a way that is simple enough for the special education student yet challenging enough even for the gifted student
- involves the whole child and doesn't rely on the traditional paper and pencil approach

- includes a variety of activities (art, movement, games, and so forth) to appeal to different learning styles and to pique student interest
- has activities that can be taught in the regular classroom or the library media center (Activities that require the use of the media center are marked with an asterisk in the title index; all others are also appropriate for the classroom.)
- provides the application, not just practice, for skills taught
- provides immediate feedback to students
- allows immediate evaluation by teacher of every student
- has materials needed for teaching ready to go so they can be quickly and easily reproduced directly from the book

One of the difficulties in teaching library research skills at the elementary level is that a media specialist sees the students only for short periods of time and usually only once a week. After the time needed for book checkout and reader guidance, there are usually only about twenty minutes left for instruction. Therefore, this book contains a cumulative series of games and activities that can fit into this twenty-minute format. You can use the book as is to establish a building-block approach to teaching library research skills, or you can dip into it as needed by using the special indexes provided in the appendix.

Looking for a way to teach the use of the card catalog, the periodical index, brainstorming, taking notes, or organizing a bibliography? See the Subject Index.

Looking for an art activity, a learning center activity to reinforce skills you have already taught, a game that will get your children up on their feet and moving? See the Art, Center, or Movement sections of the Type of Activity Index.

Perhaps you will want to find activities suitable for a particular grade level in the Grade Level Index, or establish an achievement award system with help from "Skill Roundup Awards," also found in the appendix.

Select the game or activity you want, gather the materials listed, and watch your student have fun while they learn. As one second grader summed it up for the class, "Now I can learn about anything I want to!" May all our students find that joy in becoming independent learners!

Patti Hulet

CONTENTS

GETTING TO KNOW
THE
LIBRARY
MEDIA
CENTER

LE GRAND TOUR

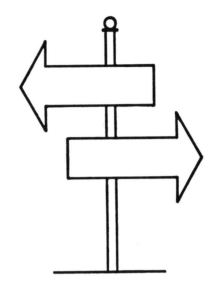

Skill Reinforced

    Awareness of the variety of resources in the library media center

Type of Activity

    Whole class movement activity

Grade Level: K–3

Time Required

    Several sessions, with a minimum of one session per area or type of equipment

Prerequisite

    None. These are among the first experiences students will have with the Library Media Center.

Materials

    A name tag or sign, if they are not already visible, could be made for each area and/or type of equipment.

Procedure

1. Let children experience the *whole* library media center (LMC). When sharing picture books, have students sit in the picture book area. When sharing a biography, perhaps one of George Washington in honor of President's Day, sit in the biography area.

2. Gradually introduce the LMC vocabulary (see hints below) and let students see where each new area is in relation to the door, the picture book area, the checkout desk, and any other areas they may be aware of. Paperbacks, magazines, reference books, the card catalog or computer terminal, and AV software and equipment are new and fascinating to most children. Even knowing where the wastebaskets and pencil sharpeners are is important in order for them to function in the LMC.

3. Introduce each area or piece of equipment and software one at a time, spending as much time as desired. The object is to continue until children have visited, and feel comfortable in, every corner of the library media center. While all students will not understand or remember everything, they will be able to catch the feeling that the LMC is a wonderful, exciting, and interesting place.

Vocabulary Hints

Biographies are books about people.
Picture books are mostly make-believe with lots of pictures to help tell the stories.
Fiction books contain longer make-believe stories without many pictures.
Nonfiction books consist of true information on all kinds of subjects.
The *reference area* is for answering questions.
Magazines are more current than books. Each issue has the same title but the inside is different.
Paperbacks are just like the hardcover editions except they have bendable covers.

Follow-up Activities

EGG HUNT
LINE 'EM UP! MOVE 'EM OUT! (may be concurrent)
CONCENTRATION
AROUND THE WORLD WITH CALL NUMBERS (depending on grade level, may be
concurrent)
MEDIA MAZE

LINE 'EM UP! MOVE 'EM OUT!

Skills Reinforced

Identifying colors
Identifying the author, title, and call number of a book
Arranging in alphabetical order

Type of Activity

Whole class movement activity

Grade Level: K–3

Time Required

A few minutes at the end of class when the story or lesson is completed and each child has checked out books

Prerequisites

Knowledge of colors and letters of the alphabet

Materials

Clothes children are wearing
Books students have checked out to read

Procedure

1. Select one or more of the following response routines that reviews concepts students have already learned.
2. Follow the suggested response routines for teaching concepts while also lining up students.

Suggested Routines

For Colors

"Stand up if you are wearing green."
"Stand up if any of your clothes have blue."
"Sit down if you are wearing yellow."
Continue with other colors until all students have had a chance to stand up and sit down.
"If you are wearing red, you may go line up at the door."
Continue with other colors. Students must be able to point to the color as they go past the leader to line up.
When most students can identify colors move on to "Suggested Routine for Colors on Book Covers."

For Colors on Book Covers

Follow the pattern established with colors on the students' clothes. The only difference is that they study the front cover of their book instead of their clothes.

For Identifying the Title of a Book

When students can correctly identify colors, show them where the title of the book is on the front cover.
"Point to the title of your book." When all students can find the title and most know their letters, move on to the next step.

"Point to the first letter of the title of your book. When I come by to check your answer, please tell me the letter name." (If a title starts with *A, An,* or *The,* have the student cover it with a hand and go on to the next word.)

After all students have been checked, have them line up in alphabetical order:

"Line up if your title starts with the letter *A.*"

"Line up if your title starts with the letter *B.*"

Remember: Students must file by so leader can check, congratulate, and offer encouragement to each student.

For Identifying Author's Name

Show students where the author's name usually is in relation to the title on the front cover. (Once in a while a book does not have the author listed on the cover; this is a good time to show the students the title page.)

"Point to the author's last name on your book."

"What letter does it start with?" (Check individually.)

Line students up by first letter of author's last name.

For Identifying Call Numbers

Show students where to find the call number on the spine of a book. "Find the call number on the spine of your book. Point to the top line." Check students.

"Stand up if the top line is a capital *E.* Sit down. Stand up if it is not an *E.* Sit down."

Students should show spines so leader can quickly check.

"Line up if the call number is EA, EB. . ."

"Line up if the call number does not have an *E* on the top line."

Variations

- Students could line up by kind of story: "Line up if your book is about an animal. Line up if it is about. . ."
- Students could "walk" a different way each visit, for example, walk on tiptoe, hop like a bunny, walk like the character in today's story or like a seasonal character (a skeleton).

Follow-up Activity

STEPPIN' TIME

EGG HUNT

Skill Reinforced

Identifying specific areas of the LMC

Type of Activity

Whole class game

Grade Level: 1–3

Time Required

One session

Prerequisite

LE GRAND TOUR

Materials

Basket

Paper eggs with questions on them, reproduced onto colored card stock, laminated, and cut out

Paper eggs for awards, reproduced onto colored paper and cut out

Procedure

1. Review all the areas and items introduced in LE GRAND TOUR (card catalog, reference area, picture books, and so on). Have students point to the area or item from where they are sitting. Be sure to include all problem areas (ones where students often get confused).

2. Scatter the eggs that have questions on them on the floor.

3. One by one, let each child select an egg from the floor. After student (or teacher) reads the question on the egg aloud, the child goes to the appropriate area or item.

4. If correct, the student places the egg in the basket and receives an egg award.

5. Let the class help a faltering child; this student can have another chance with a new question after everyone in the class has had one turn.

6. Everyone should leave with an award.

Variations

- Use other shapes and prizes: four-leaf clover with a paper or plastic coin from a treasure pot for a prize; flowers; snowflakes; leaf shapes in various colors; apples.

- This activity could be done with older students in a classroom using a transparency map of the LMC. Each student would pick an egg and locate the appropriate area on the unlabeled map.

Follow-up Activities

CONCENTRATION

MEDIA MAZE

Egg Hunt

Where are
the
dictionaries?

Egg Hunt

Where are
the picture
books?

Egg Hunt

Where are
books to be
returned?

Egg Hunt

Where are
the
magazines?

Egg Hunt

Where are
the fiction
books?

Egg Hunt

Where is the
card catalog?

Egg Hunt

Where are
the
nonfiction
books?

Egg Hunt

Where is the
reference
area?

Egg Hunt

Where are
the study
carrels?

Egg Hunt

Where is the
wastebasket?

Egg Hunt

Where are
the display
cases?

Egg Hunt

Where is the
pencil
sharpener?

Egg Hunt

Where are
the filmstrips
kept?

Egg Hunt

Where are
the
paperbacks?

Egg Hunt

Where is the
checkout
desk?

Egg Hunt

Where are
the
biographies?

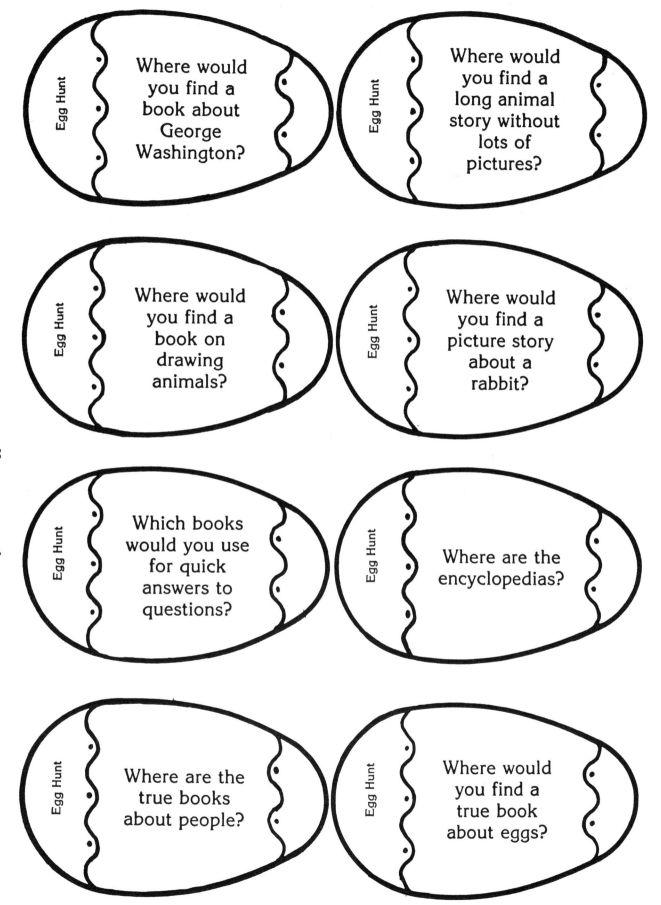

Egg Hunt
Where would you find a book about George Washington?

Egg Hunt
Where would you find a long animal story without lots of pictures?

Egg Hunt
Where would you find a book on drawing animals?

Egg Hunt
Where would you find a picture story about a rabbit?

Egg Hunt
Which books would you use for quick answers to questions?

Egg Hunt
Where are the encyclopedias?

Egg Hunt
Where are the true books about people?

Egg Hunt
Where would you find a true book about eggs?

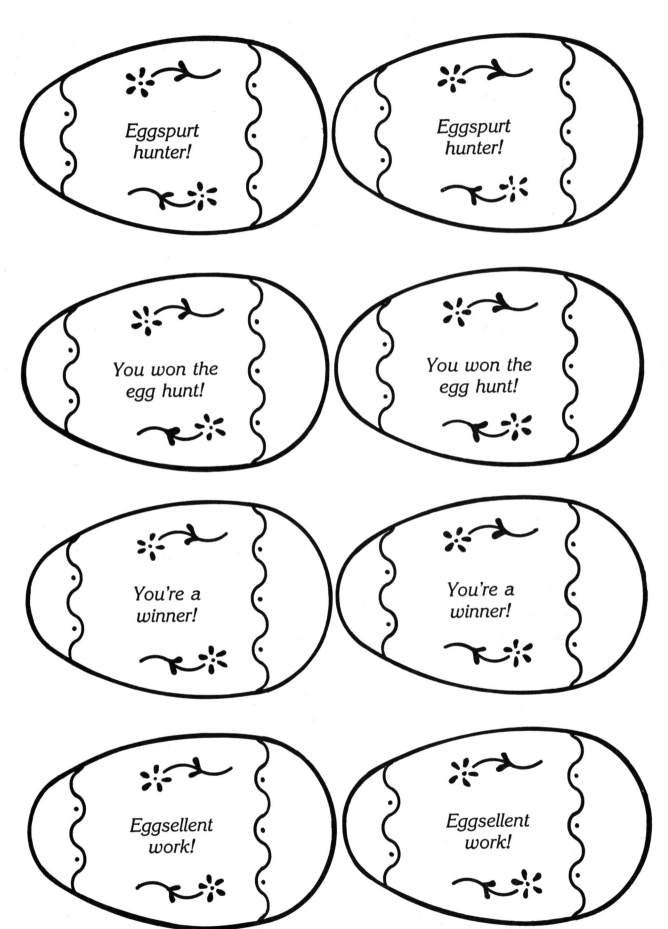

Eggspurt
hunter!

Eggspurt
hunter!

You won the
egg hunt!

You won the
egg hunt!

You're a
winner!

You're a
winner!

Eggsellent
work!

Eggsellent
work!

STEPPIN' TIME

Skills Reinforced
Visualizing concepts of drama shapes and LMC vocabulary

Type of Activity
Whole class movement activity

Grade Level: K–3

Time Required
Minimum of three sessions

Prerequisites
Introduction to LMC vocabulary used (e.g., book cover, spine, call number)
LINE 'EM UP! MOVE 'EM OUT!

Materials
Space for children to move
Record: "Seven Jumps" found on *Rhythmically Moving 2* (High/Scope, Ypsilanti, MI) or *All Purpose Folk Dances* (RCA), etc.
Record player

General Guidelines

1. Set boundaries. No student can go beyond established boundaries. If a student does, have him/her quietly sit on perimeter for a short time (until ready to act properly).
2. When teacher (leader) says, "Freeze!," everyone freezes right where they are and in the position they are in. You might want to replace this with a snap of the fingers or a clap—just be consistent.
3. When the teacher (leader) says "Relax," it means everyone is to relax with their hands at their sides right where they are standing.
4. There should be no extra "sounds," because students must listen for directions and answer questions.
5. Encourage students—they thrive on it. Say, "Betsy is making a wonderful shape! She has one arm twisted above her head and one behind her." or "I see some great shapes! All of them are different!"

Procedure

1. Use the sample routines to have students walk and form shapes in general.
2. Use the sample routines to have students practice concept shapes using the vocabulary.
3. Follow *Procedures For Putting Routines To Music.*

Sample Routines

For Practicing Walks

"Walk like a tall book."

"Walk like a short book."

"Walk like a fat book."

"Walk like a skinny book."

"Walk as if you are painting pictures with both hands."

"Walk as if you are the author, thinking and writing your book."

"Walk as if you are shaking with excitement to read the book."

"Walk like a monster."

"Walk on your tiptoes."

"Walk on the outsides of your feet."

"Walk on your heels."

"Walk like Curious George."

For Practicing Shapes in General

"What's the difference between open and closed? How do you show it with your body?"
(Closed shapes have few "holes," while open shapes have lots of lines and angles
showing.)

"Make a closed shape."

"Now make an open shape. Good!"

"Make a tightly closed shape. Open it a little with one arm. Now another arm." (Shape
does not have to be symmetrical.) "Now one leg; the other leg."

"Make a big, open shape with your whole body and hold it."

"Make another shape and hold it."

"This time make a medium, open shape." (Students should hold after each shape is
made.)

"Another one."

"Let's make a low, open shape."

"Now another one."

"Make a medium, closed shape."

"Make a different shape."

"Make a low, closed shape."

"Now make a different one."

Continue varying the level or position of the body and the openness/closedness of the
shape.

For Practicing Concept Shapes

"Think of the word *book cover*. What does a book cover do? Yes, it protects the book.
Make a shape to remind you of *book cover* and hold." (Be sure to compliment
students.)

"Our next word is *spine*. What does it do? Yes, that's right! It helps the book stand
straight and tall. Make a tall shape that reminds you of the spine of a book. Good! I
see fat spines, skinny spines. . ."

"What was our shape for book cover? Let's go back and make that shape again. Hold.
Now make your shape for spine and hold. Good. Relax."

"Our next word is *call number*. What does it do? Yes, it tells you the book's address.
Where is it? Yes, near the bottom of the spine. Make a low, closed shape to remind
you of *call number*."

Review shapes for book cover, spine, and call number.

"What is on the top line of the call number? That's right, a capital *E*. What does *E* stand for? *Easy*, yes. *Everybody*, yes. The section in the library; great! Make a big open shape to stand for the section of the library. Now make a shape that says, *E is for everybody!* Hold it!"

Review book cover, spine, call number, top line is for section, and *E*.

"What does the bottom line of the call number represent? That's right, it is the first letter of the author's last name. Make a shape for the bottom line as author."

Review book cover, spine, call number, top line is for section, *E*, and author.

"What order do these books go in? That's right! Alphabetical order. We are going to make three quick shapes: one for A, then B, then the letter C. Think of a shape for each. Now make a shape to remind you of A; hold. A shape for B; hold. And a shape for C; hold."

"Let's put it all together! I'll put the music on."

Procedure for Putting Routines to Music

1. Review walks and concept shapes. Students do not have to make the same shapes they made in other sessions.

2. Tell students that they will walk in various ways as the teacher directs while the music is playing and that they will make shapes for the library vocabulary, which they are to hold on the long notes.

3. Using the suggested list below, lead students through the dance. Note, the book cover shape is the only shape held the first time. A long note will be added each time the music gets to that part. That means you will repeat the shape(s) and add a new one each time.

WALKS	SHAPES FOR HOLDS
tall	book cover
short	spine
fat	call number
skinny	top line is section
on tiptoe	E is for everybody
on outside of feet	bottom line is for author
on inside of feet	ABC order

4. The first time through the dance, ask students, "What shape are you holding?" "What does it do?" and, if appropriate, "Where is it?" The second time, have them whisper the answers. The third time they should think the shape and its meaning as they do the dance.

Variations

• Students may move freely around the room for the walks, or the leader may prefer to have students walk in a circle around the room.

• Concept shapes can be repeated any number of times with the same or other vocabulary/library concepts being added.

Follow-up Activity

WE'VE GOT RHYTHM

CONCENTRATION

Skill Reinforced

Review of LMC vocabulary

Type of Activity

Whole class game

Grade Level: 1–4

Time Required

Depending on the class, two games can be played in one session

Prerequisites

Knowledge of LMC vocabulary
LE GRAND TOUR

Materials

Concentration gameboard, made of two poster boards and thirty numbered library pockets (see picture above)
Transparency of *Library Notes*
Concentration game cards, reproduced onto colored cardstock and laminated
Sixty construction paper markers in two colors, one color for each team (thirty of each color)

Procedure

1. Review areas of the LMC and vocabulary using the transparency. Show the students the word cards that match the picture cards. (Note: matching game cards have the same letter of the alphabet on them. Students do not have to be able to read the words to play the game; remember, the vocabulary is still being introduced.

2. Mix up the word and picture cards and place one in each pocket upside down.

3. Divide the class into two teams. Each team is to match as many picture cards with their appropriate word cards as possible.

4. Each student takes a turn being responsible for giving two numbers; teammates may quietly help. When the student calls out the numbers, the cards are turned over revealing their contents.

5. If no match is made, the cards are returned to the pockets upside down. If a match is made, the cards are removed and colored markers for that team are placed in the pockets. The team continues until it misses; then the other team takes a turn.

6. The team with the most colored markers wins the game.

Variations

- Add more card sets with additional vocabulary and picture matches.
- Let the students draw their own pictures for pictorial reminders of the LMC areas and vocabulary. Each time the game is played, a different student's work can be displayed.

Follow-up Activity

MEDIA MAZE

LIBRARY NOTES

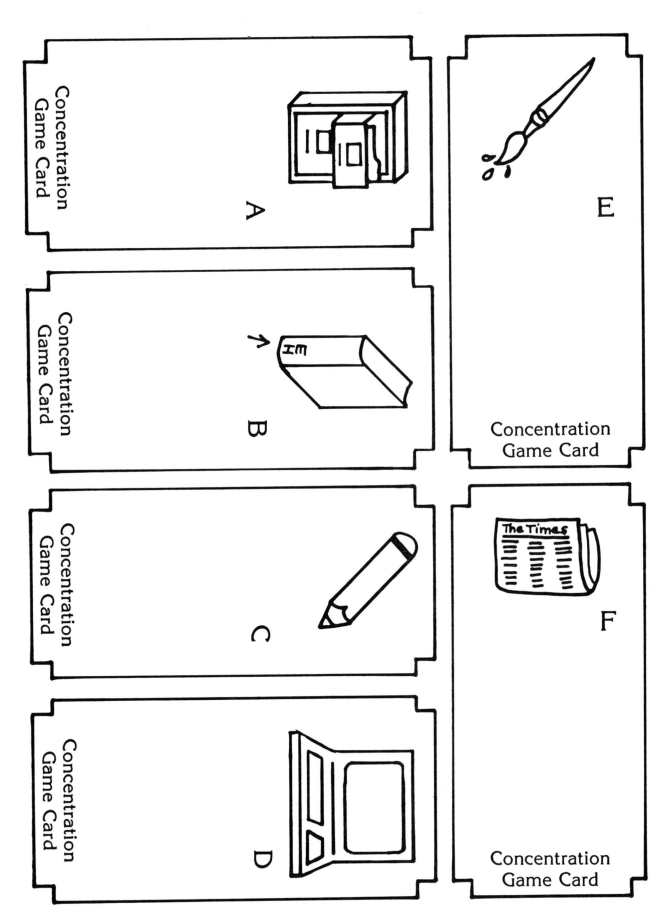

Concentration Game Card A

Concentration Game Card B

Concentration Game Card C

Concentration Game Card D

Concentration Game Card E

Concentration Game Card F

A

vertical
file

Concentration
Game Card

B

call
number

Concentration
Game Card

C

author

Concentration
Game Card

D

computer
terminal

Concentration
Game Card

E

illustrator

Concentration
Game Card

F

newspaper

Concentration
Game Card

Concentration Game Card — G

Sesame Street
National Geographic
Rangers

Concentration Game Card — H

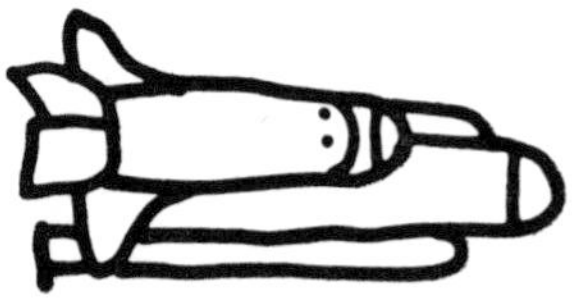

Concentration Game Card — I

Concentration Game Card — J

Winnie the Pooh

Concentration Game Card — K

Concentration Game Card — L

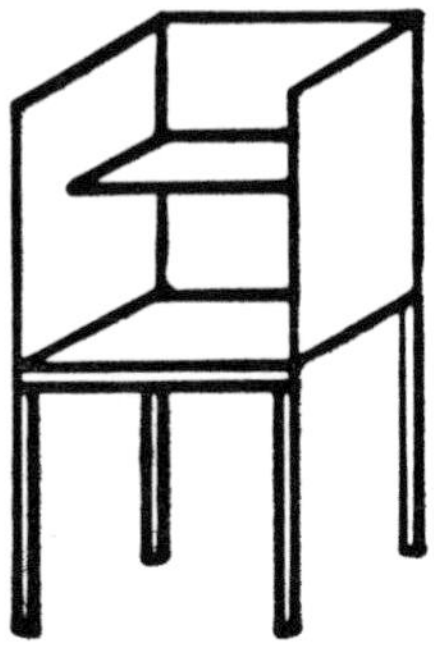

Concentration Game Card

Concentration Game Card

card
catalog

K

Concentration
Game Card

magazines

G

Concentration
Game Card

nonfiction

H

Concentration
Game Card

study
carrel

L

Concentration
Game Card

fiction

I

Concentration
Game Card

title

J

Concentration
Game Card

Concentration
Game Card

M

biography

N

Concentration
Game Card

N

Concentration
Game Card

Concentration
Game Card

listening
center

O

Concentration
Game Card

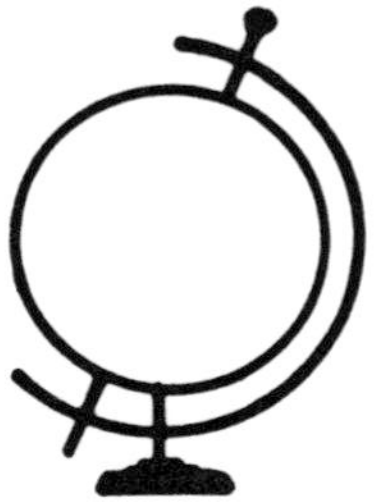

O

Concentration
Game Card

M

globe

Concentration
Game Card

Concentration
Game Card

Concentration
Game Card

Concentration
Game Card

Concentration
Game Card

Concentration
Game Card

Concentration
Game Card

Concentration
Game Card

Concentration
Game Card

FAIRY TALE CODES

Skill Reinforced
Using alphabetical order

Type of Activity
Whole class, small group, partners, or individual
paper and pencil or game (see variations)

Grade Level: 1+

Time Required
One session

Prerequisite
Knowledge of the alphabet
(codes use preceding or following letters)

Materials
Fairy Tale Code Cards A–F
Paper
Pencils

Procedure

1. Divide class into small groups of two to four
   children each.
2. Distribute a Fairy Tale Code Card, paper, and
   pencil to each group.
3. Explain that "a" is the letter that comes after
   "z" and that "z" is the letter that precedes "a."
4. Let students decipher the coded titles and check
   answers against the answer key.

Variations

- Use Nursery Rhyme Code Cards (cards G–L).
- Using book titles or author's and illustrator's names,
  make additional code cards with answer keys; or let
  students make them.
- Write coded titles on the blackboard or a transparency.
  Have students decode the title and raise their hands as
  soon as they have the answer. When most students have
  their hands raised, call on one to give the answer. This
  could be used in a contest situation, giving a point to
  the team that answers correctly first.

FAIRY TALE CODE CARD   A

Write the letter that comes before the letter given.

1. Sbqvoafm
2. Cfbvuz boe uif Cfbtu
3. Djoefsfmmb
4. Qvtt jo Cpput

FAIRY TALE CODE CARD   B

Write the letter that comes before the letter given.

1. Topx Xijuf
2. Uif Gsph Qsjodf
3. Uisff Mjuumf Qjht
4. Uif Tufbegbtu Ujo Tpmejfs

FAIRY TALE CODE CARD   C

Write the letter that comes before the letter given.

1. Kbdl boe uif Cfbotubml
2. Uif Fmwft boe uif Tipfnblfs
3. Uif Qsjodftt boe uif Qfb
4. Ibotfm boe Hsfufm

FAIRY TALE CODE CARD   D

Write the letter that comes after the letter given.

1. Sgd Sgqdd Khsskd Ohfr
2. Qzotmydk
3. Sgd Eqnf Oqhmbd
4. Otrr hm Annsr

FAIRY TALE CODE CARD   E

Write the letter that comes after the letter given.

1. Sgd Dkudr zmc sgd Rgndlzjdq
2. Sgd Fhmfdqaqdzc Lzm
3. Adztsx zmc sgd Adzrs
4. Gzmrdk zmc Fqdsdk

FAIRY TALE CODE CARD   F

Write the letter that comes after the letter given.

1. Sgd Rsdzcezrs Shm Rnkchdq
2. Rmnv Vghsd
3. Izbj zmc sgd Adzmrszkj
4. Sgd Tfkx Ctbjkhmf

NURSERY RHYME CODE CARD G

Write the letter that comes before the letter given.

1. Mjuumf Cp-Qffq
2. Pme Npuifs Ivccbse
3. Uifsf Xbt b Dspplfe Nbo
4. Mjuumf Cpz Cmvf

NURSERY RHYME CODE CARD J

Write the letter that comes before the letter given.

1. Ifz Ejeemf Ejeemf
2. Ju't Sbjojoh, Ju't Qpvsjoh!
3. Ijdlpsz, Ejdlpsz, Epdl!
4. Tjnqmf Tjnpo

NURSERY RHYME CODE CARD H

Write the letter that comes after the letter given.

1. Hs'r Qzhmhmf, Hs'r Ontqhmf!
2. Khsskd Anx Aktd
3. Sgdqd Vzr z Bqnnjdc Lzm
4. Nkc Lnsgdq Gtaazqc

NURSERY RHYME CODE CARD K

Write the letter that comes after the letter given.

1. Sgdqd Vzr zm Nkc Vnlzm
2. Rhlokd Rhlnm
3. Gdx Chcckd Chcckd
4. Ghbjnqx, Chbjnqx, Cnbj!

NURSERY RHYME CODE CARD I

Write the letter that comes after the letter given.

1. Sgqdd Akhmc Lhbd
2. Svhmjkd, Svhmjkd Khsskd Rszq
3. Khsskd Lhrr Lteeds
4. Khsskd An-Oddo

NURSERY RHYME CODE CARD L

Write the letter that comes before the letter given.

1. Mjuumf Njtt Nvggfu
2. Uisff Cmjoe Njdf
3. Uifsf Xbt bo Pme Xpnbo
4. Uxjolmf, Uxjolmf Mjuumf Tubs

FAIRY TALE CODES (answer key)

Card A (preceding letter)

1. Rapunzel
2. Beauty and the Beast
3. Cinderella
4. Puss in Boots

Card B (preceding letter)

1. Snow White
2. The Frog Prince
3. Three Little Pigs
4. The Steadfast Tin Soldier

Card C (preceding letter)

1. Jack and the Beanstalk
2. The Elves and the Shoemaker
3. The Princess and the Pea
4. Hansel and Gretel

Card D (following letter)

1. The Three Little Pigs
2. Rapunzel
3. The Frog Prince
4. Puss in Boots

Card E (following letter)

1. The Elves and the Shoemaker
2. The Gingerbread Man
3. Beauty and the Beast
4. Hansel and Gretel

Card F (following letter)

1. The Steadfast Tin Soldier
2. Snow White
3. Jack and the Beanstalk
4. The Ugly Duckling

NURSERY RHYME CODES (answer key)

Card G (preceding letter)

1. Little Bo-Peep
2. Old Mother Hubbard
3. There Was a Crooked Man
4. Little Boy Blue

Card H (following letter)

1. It's Raining, It's Pouring!
2. Little Boy Blue
3. There Was a Crooked Man
4. Old Mother Hubbard

Card I (following letter)

1. Three Blind Mice
2. Twinkle, Twinkle Little Star
3. Little Miss Muffet
4. Little Bo-Peep

Card J (preceding letter)

1. Hey Diddle Diddle
2. It's Raining, It's Pouring!
3. Hickory, Dickory, Dock!
4. Simple Simon

Card K (following letter)

1. There Was an Old Woman
2. Simple Simon
3. Hey Diddle Diddle
4. Hickory, Dickory, Dock!

Card L (preceding letter)

1. Little Miss Muffet
2. Three Blind Mice
3. There Was an Old Woman
4. Twinkle, Twinkle Little Star

WE'VE GOT RHYTHM

Skill Reinforced

Recognizing LMC vocabulary orally

Type of Activity

Whole class movement activity

Grade Level: 2+

Time Required

Varies from five minutes to a full session depending on student interest and amount of vocabulary

Prerequisites

Introduction to LMC vocabulary used (biography, encyclopedia, card catalog)
LE GRAND TOUR
STEPPIN' TIME

Materials

Cards with the vocabulary words written on them, if desired

Procedure for Rhythm Pattern

1. Select the vocabulary students are to learn (see samples below).
2. Say the first vocabulary word. Have the students orally repeat the word. Say the next word and have students repeat it. Have students repeat the two words in the word chain.
3. Continue adding words and repeating the growing chain. Four or five words is enough at first, as beginning students will not be able to handle the whole list.
4. Have the students say the first word in the chain and practice putting the rhythm pattern (see below) with each syllable. Repeat the complete word chain, adding the rhythm pattern for the first word.
5. Continue through the list introducing one rhythm pattern at a time. Each time be sure students repeat all the words and rhythm patterns previously learned.
6. Have the students say the word chain with accompanying rhythm patterns using a variety of voices (high, deep, squeaky). Also be sure to vary the tempo.

Procedure for Motion

Start the word chain as for the rhythm pattern. Instead of putting one movement with each syllable, one free-form motion (see samples below) is used for the whole word.

Sample Rhythm Patterns and Motions

Word	Rhythm Pattern	Motion
library	both hands pat knees, shoulders, and then reach high in the air	open arms out wide
globe	finger in air circles once	roll hands
map	two fingers in air (one from each hand) to form circle	hand makes waving motion

encyclopedia	with chopping motions, alternate left and right hands to simulate a row of books on a shelf: en cy clo pe di a L R L R L R	bring hands in as if holding a load of books
card catalog	slide hands together for each syllable	pretend to rock a tray in arms
fiction	scissor hands in front, alternating the one on top	wave finger of one hand in air
nonfiction	hit fists together, alternating the one on top	fist raised high in the air
biography	make small circle with finger; hold hand vertically; slant hands high; slant hands low (make stick person in air)	bring one hand to face as if thinking
magazine	fists alternate in and out in front of body	move head from one side to the other side
reference	one hand out, then in; then with hands together, open like a book	hands together rotate so other hand is on top
audio-visual	three finger taps at ears, then tap above, under, and to side of each eye carefully	point to ears then make circles around eyes with forefingers and thumbs

Variations

- Let the students determine the order for the word chain, perhaps even the vocabulary to be included.
- Let the students come up with their own rhythm patterns or motions for each word in the word chain.
- Use other words in the chain and create rhythm patterns and motions for each word.
- As the class says the word chain, one half of the students can do the rhythm pattern, the other half the motions; then reverse.

Note: If this activity is done with younger children (K–1), it is best to have students do a motion for each word in the chain. Rhythm and syllabication are appropriate for second grade and above.

Follow-up Activities

CONCENTRATION
RIDDLE CHANTS
MEDIA CENTER MAZE

AROUND THE WORLD WITH CALL NUMBERS

Skill Reinforced

Recognizing different categories of call numbers quickly

Type of Activity

Whole class game

Grade Level: 2+

Prerequisite/Concurrent

LE GRAND TOUR

Time Required

One session plus, depending on student interest

Materials

Around the World cards

Pregame Activity

1. Check the Around the World cards provided to make sure they match the call number system used in the LMC (92 or B designates biography). Make any corrections or additions as necessary on a copy of the blank cards included.
2. Hold up one Around the World card at a time and have the entire class say aloud which section of the LMC is represented by the call number shown.
3. Give hints such as "NONfiction has NUMbers," as necessary.
4. When most of the class recognizes the various call numbers and is able to name the categories, it is time to start the game.

Game Play

1. Have the students sit on the floor in two rows facing you.
2. Have two players stand (start on one end of either row).
3. Show an Around the World card.
4. The first one of the pair to correctly name the kind of call number wins. The losing player sits down and the next player stands. The winner moves to the next player and competes with him.
5. The faster player continues until someone is even speedier. Then he sits in that person's place, and the new winner moves on.
6. Play continues on across the one row and then across the other. Proceed until all students have had a turn or until one player completes an entire round.

Variations

- Add more cards for other types of materials and sections of the LMC.
- Play while students are standing in lines waiting to leave the LMC or classroom.

Note: Students enjoy this game and ask for it often. Use it or the pregame activity when a time-filler is needed, because it makes a good review.

Follow-up Activity

WHAT'S MY POSITION?

398.2 Aes Around the World	398.2 Ful Around the World	398.2 Gri Around the World
398.6 Mot Around the World	582 Zim Around the World	599 Gri Around the World
599 Ste Around the World	551.4 Des Around the World	551.4 Sto Around the World

551.6 Erb Around the World	598.1 Wol Around the World	598.2 Sto Around the World
796.4 Bre Around the World	796.4 Des Around the World	917.2 Sch Around the World
917.45 Abe Around the World	917.41 Was Around the World	917.5 Tre Around the World

636.08 Hor Around the World	636.7 Pet Around the World	636.13 Tig Around the World
398.6 Bab Around the World	808.81 Lio Around the World	811 Fer Around the World
292 Myt Around the World	978 Pit Around the World	636.2 Ged Around the World

E A Around the World	E B Around the World	E C Around the World
E C Around the World	E D Around the World	E F Around the World
E G Around the World	E H Around the World	E K Around the World

E L Around the World	E M Around the World	E N Around the World
E P Around the World	E P Around the World	E Q Around the World
E R Around the World	E S Around the World	E S Around the World

E T Around the World	E T Around the World	E U Around the World
E V Around the World	E W Around the World	E Z Around the World
E D Around the World	E E Around the World	E H Around the World

Fic Ada	Fic Aik	Fic Ale
Around the World	Around the World	Around the World
Fic Cla	Fic Cle	Fic Clo
Around the World	Around the World	Around the World
Fic Coa	Fic Con	Fic Coo
Around the World	Around the World	Around the World

Fic Ear Around the World	Fic Est Around the World	Fic Kje Around the World
Fic Geo Around the World	Fic Ger Around the World	Fic Hay Around the World
Fic Bod Around the World	Fic Bos Around the World	Fic Bre Around the World

Fic Sto Around the World	**Fic Ras** Around the World	**Fic Raw** Around the World
Fic Rou Around the World	**Fic Whi** Around the World	**Fic Wys** Around the World
Fic Tre Around the World	**Fic Tra** Around the World	**Fic Tru** Around the World

92 **Ada** Around the World	**92** **Pow** Around the World	**92** **Sac** Around the World
92 **Rev** Around the World	**92** **Roc** Around the World	**92** **Roo** Around the World
92 **Jac** Around the World	**92** **Jef** Around the World	**92** **Joh** Around the World

92 Tub	92 Tru	92 Bla
Around the World	Around the World	Around the World
92 For	92 Gre	92 Fra
Around the World	Around the World	Around the World
92 Rea	92 Poc	92 Bus
Around the World	Around the World	Around the World

92 **Mos** Around the World	**92** **Moz** Around the World	**92** **Mac** Around the World
92 **Mar** Around the World	**92** **Dis** Around the World	**92** **Hen** Around the World
92 **Hit** Around the World	**92** **Kin** Around the World	**92** **Kis** Around the World

Ref 031 Wor Around the World	Ref 031 Ame Around the World	Ref 028.5 Chi Around the World
Ref 582 Cac Around the World	Ref 979.17 Our Around the World	Ref 979.1 Wag Around the World
Ref 979.15 Rim Around the World	Ref 050 Ser Around the World	Ref 780.6 Son Around the World

Ref 508 Oxf Around the World	Ref 595.7 Enc Around the World	Ref 589.2 Dug Around the World
Ref 598.2 Fie Around the World	Ref 591 Grz Around the World	Ref 549 Min Around the World
Ref 574 Com Around the World	Ref 507.8 Sci Around the World	Ref 342.97 Ari Around the World

Ref 808.81 Wor Around the World	Ref 808.81 Ind Around the World	Ref 808.81 Sub Around the World
Ref 808.82 Ral Around the World	Ref 808.88 Bar Around the World	Ref 920 Dic Around the World
Ref 920 Gal Around the World	Ref 594 Sea Around the World	Ref 028.12 Kin Around the World

Around
the World

Around
the World

Around
the World

Around
the World

Around
the World

Around
the World

Around
the World

Around
the World

Around
the World

WHAT'S MY POSITION?

Skill Reinforced

Practice putting call numbers in shelf order

Type of Activity

Whole class game

Grade Level: 2+

Time Required

Two sessions minimum

Prerequisites

STEPPIN' TIME
AROUND THE WORLD

Materials

Around the World cards
What's My Position section labels

Procedure

1. Pull all the Around the World cards with nonfiction call numbers.
2. Divide the class in half, each half sitting on one side of you (positions A and B).
3. Give cards to two members from each team. Let them start lines C and D for their teams. The team members in line C and D should be in call number order.
4. Add a new player to a team as soon as its members are standing straight in line.
5. Award points as follows:
   one point to the quietest team
   one point for each correct answer
   one point to first team to finish

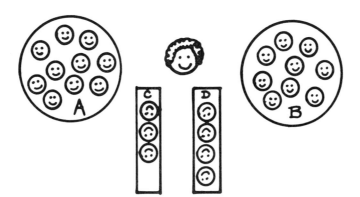

6. Play the game as many times as time or interest allows. Select a different library section to concentrate on at each visit. It will be necessary to make additional Around the World cards if a section other than nonfiction is used. Make sure a good selection of "tough" cards is included, with call numbers that are close because of alphabetical or Dewey Decimal order. For example, the Easy section needs a set of call numbers without every letter of the alphabet being represented but with duplicates of some letters. This makes the students think.

7. When students can comfortably line up in shelf order for each section (easy, fiction, nonfiction, and biography), place What's My Position? section labels on the floor.

8. Hand an Around the World card from any section to each student and allow them to line up in the correct section in the correct order (see illustration). If score is kept, it should be a class score earned for being quiet and the number of correct answers.

Easy	Fiction	Nonfiction	Biography	Reference

Follow-up Activity

Have students take partners. Give each set of partners a card and let them find the call number on a book on a library shelf. Have students raise their hands when they find the call number or can tell where it should be. If correct, hand students a new number. If incorrect, give them hints until they find it.

Warning: This can be a noisy activity because the children get excited when they find the call number.

Easy

Fiction

Nonfiction

Reference

Biography

RIDDLE CHANTS

Skill Reinforced

Recognizing LMC vocabulary

Type of Activity

Whole class movement activity

Grade Level: 1+

Time Required

Varies; from five minutes to a full session depending on
student interest and amount of vocabulary

Prerequisites

Introduction to LMC vocabulary used
(author, illustrator, title page)
WE'VE GOT RHYTHM

Materials

Chalkboard and chalk

Procedure

1. Review the vocabulary to be used. At first list the vocabulary on the chalkboard so
   students can look to find the answer while doing the activity. Later it should be
   necessary to list only new vocabulary on the board.
2. The teacher and the students set the beat by patting their knees and saying "what,
   what, what. . ." When the beat is established, everyone chants the chorus.
3. While continuing the beat, the teacher gives a clue and the class responds with the
   answer (see samples below). Continue alternating clues and answers to the beat.
   The chorus can be repeated between each set, if desired.
4. Older children should be able to play leader and give clues for the class to answer.

Choruses

I am in the media center,	or	I am in a library book,
Media center, media center.		A library book, a library book.
I am in the media center;		I am in a library book;
Guess what I am now!		Guess what I am now!

Sample Clues

I wrote the book.
I drew the pictures in the book.
I am the paper wrapped around
  the book.
I am wrapped around the book.
I tell who wrote the book.
I list the chapters in a book.
I give the information.
I am a picture in a book.
I explain the special words in a book.
I tell the subjects in the book.
I make the book stand straight.

Answers

I am the author.
I am the illustrator.
I am the jacket.

I am the book cover.
I am the title page.
I am the table of contents.
I am a chapter in a book.
I am an illustration.
I am the glossary.
I am the index.
I am the spine.

I tell where the book belongs in the library.	I am the call number.
I am the person in the book.	I am a character.
I am the message of the book.	I am the theme.
I am where and when the book takes place.	I am the setting.
I am the story plan.	I am the plot.
I am the high point of the story.	I am the climax.
I am a book about a real person.	I am a biography.
I am a book about real things.	I am a nonfiction book.
I am a book you go to for quick answers.	I am a reference book.
I am the name of a book.	I am the title.

Variations

- Let a student set the pace by starting the beat.
- Set the beat using a drum or other rhythm instrument.
- Distribute cards with either answers, clues, or both written on them. After the beat is established, a student gives what is on a card and the class gives the opposite, that is, a clue for an answer and an answer for a clue. Continue until each student has had a turn.

Follow-up Activity
WRITING ON THE WALL

WRITING ON THE WALL

Skill Reinforced

Recognizing LMC vocabulary

Type of Activity

Whole class movement activity

Grade Level: 3+

Time Required

One session

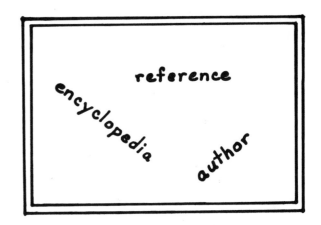

Prerequisites

Introduction to LMC vocabulary used (for example, author, nonfiction, reference)
RIDDLE CHANTS

Materials

Two sets of word cards, including all vocabulary desired

Procedure

1. Select the vocabulary the students are to use. Prepare two sets of vocabulary cards.

2. Divide the class into two teams and have each team line up. The first person in each team will be the "writer." The writers can write on opposite ends of the chalkboard or if lap boards or clipboards with paper are available, they could write on those.

3. The second person in each line is given identical word cards. They are to "write" the word one letter at a time with a finger on the back of the first person, who then writes each letter on the chalkboard. Gently scratching the back of the person in front means to erase that letter.

4. When the word is completely and correctly written down on the chalkboard, the first person turns around and says the word out loud; the team repeats it. The first team to say the word correctly wins the point.

5. Continue the game by having the first person go to the end of the line. The second person now becomes the writer.

6. Since many students need to wait, points can also be given for the team that waits most quietly.

Variation

- Using the clues from RIDDLE CHANTS, make up two sets of clue cards. The second person reads the clue, must think of the answer, and then correctly spell the word on the back of the person in front. Points should only be given for correctly spelled answers.

MEDIA CENTER MAZE

Skills Reinforced

Locating sections in the LMC using a map
Following directions

Type of Activity

Whole class art activity
Center (see Follow-up Activities)

Grade Level: 3–6

Time Required

One session minimum

Prerequisites

LE GRAND TOUR
RESEARCH IMAGERY, if desired

Materials

Map of school library media center (see sample on next page)
Transparency of map
Overhead projector
Colored markers for transparency
Photocopies of map
Crayons

Procedure

1. Draw a simple map of the school library media center. Include details such as doors and pencil sharpeners. Do not label anything by name, but items and areas may each be given a number.

2. Make a transparency of the map for classroom teacher use and reproduce copies for the students to use.

3. Distribute copies of the map to the students.

4. Let students follow along on their maps as directions are given by the teacher. At first have students identify the item or section by number, for example, state which section is represented by number eight, or what number denotes the card catalog?

5. When students are adept, have them use crayons to mark paths as designated by the teacher. The teacher may give some examples on the transparency before students mark on their maps. Examples of directions include: "Use the color blue to show the path we would take to go from the entrance to the card catalog. Use green to go from the card catalog to the nonfiction section. Let yellow show us going from the nonfiction section to the checkout desk."

6. Older students could have lots of lines criss-crossing on their maps.

Note: This activity is best done in the regular classroom. Students tend to be much more observant the next time they go to the LMC after having been required to visualize the reality of the place using only memory and a map.

Variations

- Draw a map of the public library including special features such as the microfiche and periodical sections. Use it in the same way.

Follow-up Activities

A center activity could be made with the map and an answer sheet for identifying the items and sections numbered (or lettered) on the map. Be sure to label everything with different numbers from those used in the class so students don't just remember the number and not look at the map.

Students could write up directions for a Media Center Maze excursion, perhaps based on a RESEARCH IMAGERY experience. For example, "The student enters the LMC, walks over to the reference area, gets the index to an encyclopedia, sits at a table, walks over to the globe to locate a continent in relation to ours, puts the index back on the shelf, goes to the card catalog, locates a book in nonfiction (specifically, an animal book), and walks to the checkout desk and out the door back to the classroom." The teacher could read these to the class and have the students show the path on their own maps.

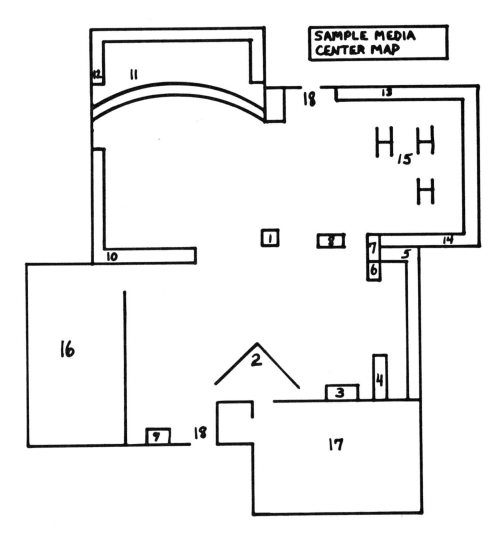

USING REFERENCE SOURCES

PUT HUMPTY DUMPTY TOGETHER EGGS-ACTLY!

Skill Reinforced

Matching a reference book with the type of information it contains

Type of Activity

Whole class game

Grade Level: 3–6

Time Required

Two sessions minimum

Prerequisite

Introduction to reference sources to be used in games

Materials

Humpty Dumpty eggs reproduced onto cardstock, cut out and in half (laminate, if desired)

Reference books that have been included in the game:
dictionary, encyclopedia volume, almanac, atlas, geographical dictionary, thesaurus, telephone book, calendar, *TV Guide*, newspaper, *Webster's Biographical Dictionary*, *Guinness Book of World Records*, *National Geographic Index*, *Bartlett's Familiar Quotations*, *Facts about the Presidents*, *Famous First Facts*, *Junior Book of Authors*, *Readers' Guide*

Humpty Dumpty's Wall cards (see answer key for reference sources included)

I.M.A. Booksnoop's Amazing, Astounding, Astonishing Library Skills Kit by Elaine Prizzi and Jeanne Hoffman, Pitman Learning, Inc., 1983.

Procedure for Matching Eggs (first session)

1. Select reference sources to be included in the game and prepare appropriate egg halves.

2. Review each reference source and discuss the type of information it contains.

3. Distribute paper eggshell halves to the students.

4. Have the students line up in two lines facing each other. One line of students should have the reference sources and the other line should have the definitions.

5. Start down the source line one at a time, having a student read the name of the reference on his or her egg half.

6. The student with the correct definition in the other line should read the definition and then test whether the egg halves match. The two students should remain standing together.

7. Continue until all sources and definitions have been matched.

8. Play the game again, but this time have the definitions read first so students must match the source titles.

Procedure for Humpty Dumpty's Wall (second session)

1. Set out the reference sources to be included so all the students can see them.

2. Quickly review with the students the type of information each contains.

3. Distribute the Humpty Dumpty's Wall cards (some students may have two) and tell students that they will be building a wall for Humpty Dumpty with the cards.

4. The student with question 1 starts. After reading the question aloud, the student brings the card up and places it on or beside the source that would most likely answer the question. If the answer is incorrect, let the student select someone to help find the right source and explain to the class why it is a better choice.

5. Continue until all the question cards have been placed.

Note: Students have difficulty distinguishing the difference between the atlas and the geographical dictionary. A simple explanation is to tell them that if the answer can be found on a map, use an atlas; an answer to any other question about a place will probably be in a geographical dictionary.

Answers to Humpty Dumpty's Wall

1, 13, 25 thesaurus
2, 14, 26 phone book
3, 15, 27 encyclopedia
4, 16, 28 atlas
5, 17, 29 biographical dictionary
6, 18, 30 dictionary

7, 19, 31 calendar
8, 20, 32 *TV Guide*
9, 21, 33 *Guinness Book of World Records*
10, 22, 34 geographical dictionary
11, 23, 35 newspaper
12, 24, 36 *Famous First Facts*

Variations

• Add more reference books and vary the descriptions on the eggs (for example, the dictionary could have several matches). Just make sure the "cracks" are different so no wrong matches occur.

• Add more questions for Humpty Dumpty's Wall to cover additional reference sources.

• Let each student have his or her own set of egg halves with which to practice.

• Mix up all the egg halves and distribute one to each student. Let students find an appropriate partner, sit down at their "station or wall" with the reference book, and look at it (or answer questions about it) until all pairs are matched. Pick up shells and distribute again to different students. Repeat as long as there is interest or time.

• Several kinds of each type of reference book can be at each "station or wall" so students can see the variety and know there are more than one available.

• While students are seated at the "wall," they could answer questions about the book:
Where is the table of contents?
Where is the index?
How is it arranged? alphabetically? by subject order? chronologically?
Which of these questions could be answered with this book?
(List four or five reference questions.)

Follow-up Activities

Set up centers for students to practice using each of the reference books.
Have students complete pages from *I.M.A. Booksnoop.*
WHO'S GOT THE ANSWER?
REFERENCE RACE

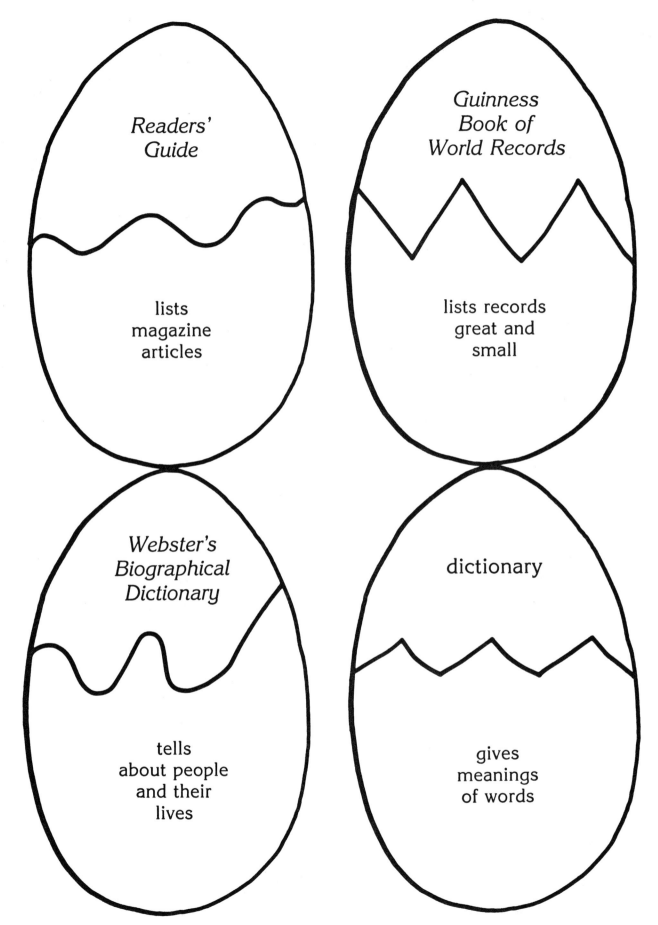

Readers'
Guide

lists
magazine
articles

Guinness
Book of
World Records

lists records
great and
small

Webster's
Biographical
Dictionary

tells
about people
and their
lives

dictionary

gives
meanings
of words

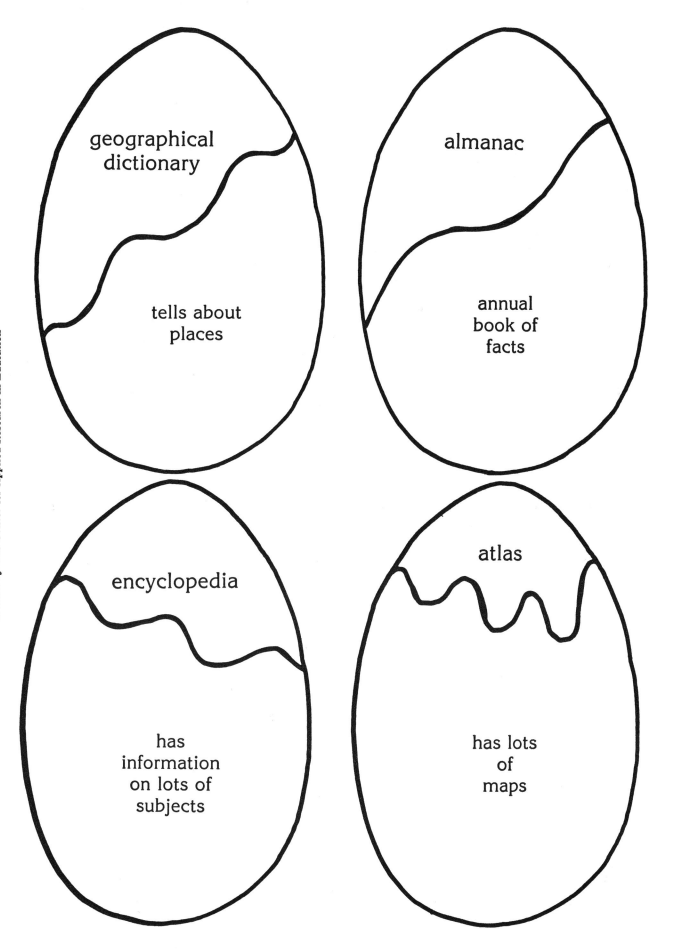

geographical
dictionary

tells about
places

almanac

annual
book of
facts

encyclopedia

has
information
on lots of
subjects

atlas

has lots
of
maps

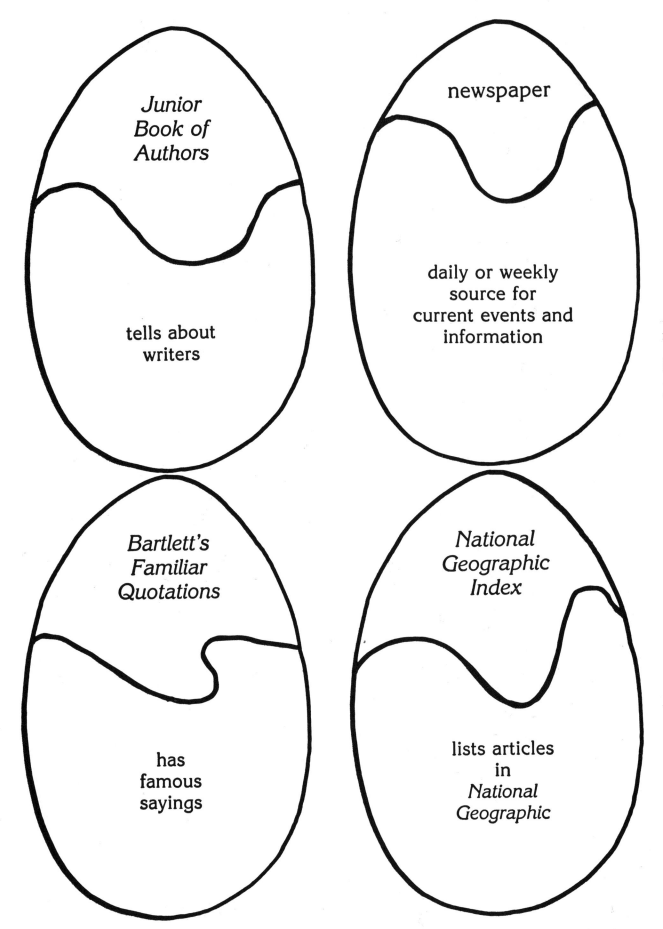

Junior
Book of
Authors

tells about
writers

newspaper

daily or weekly
source for
current events and
information

Bartlett's
Familiar
Quotations

has
famous
sayings

National
Geographic
Index

lists articles
in
National
Geographic

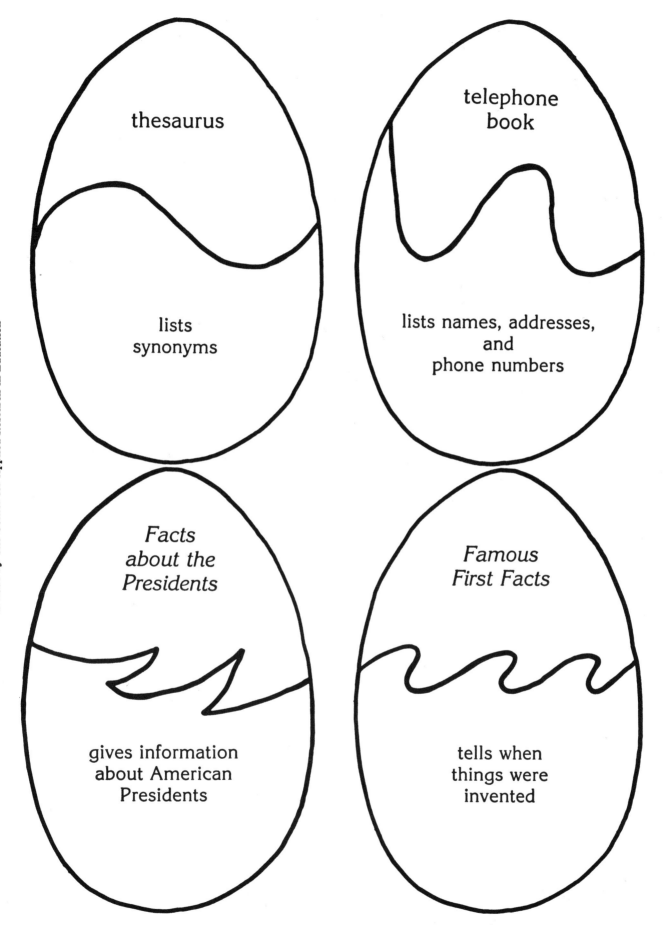

thesaurus

lists synonyms

telephone book

lists names, addresses, and phone numbers

Facts about the Presidents

gives information about American Presidents

Famous First Facts

tells when things were invented

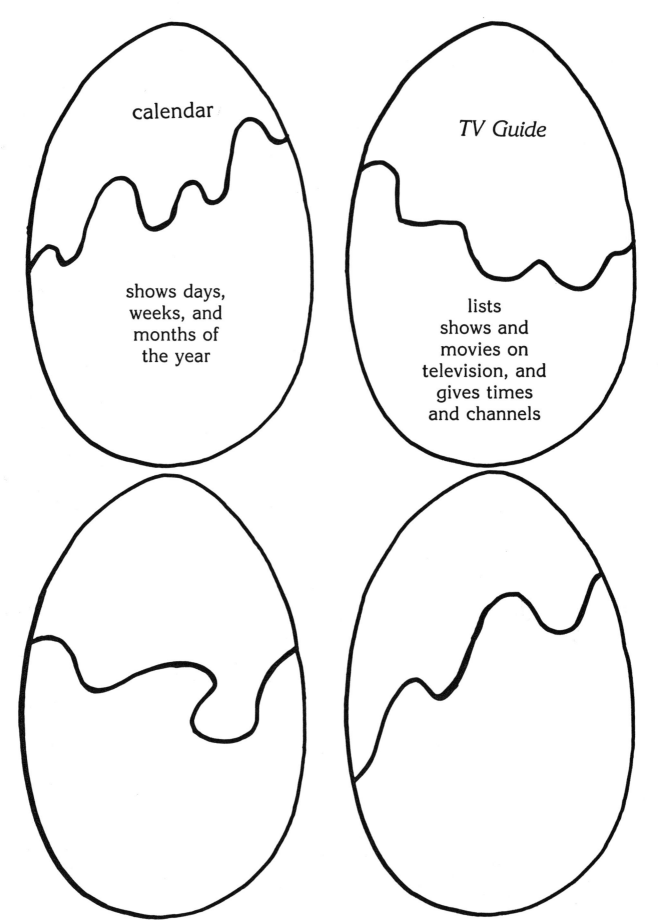

calendar

shows days, weeks, and months of the year

TV Guide

lists shows and movies on television, and gives times and channels

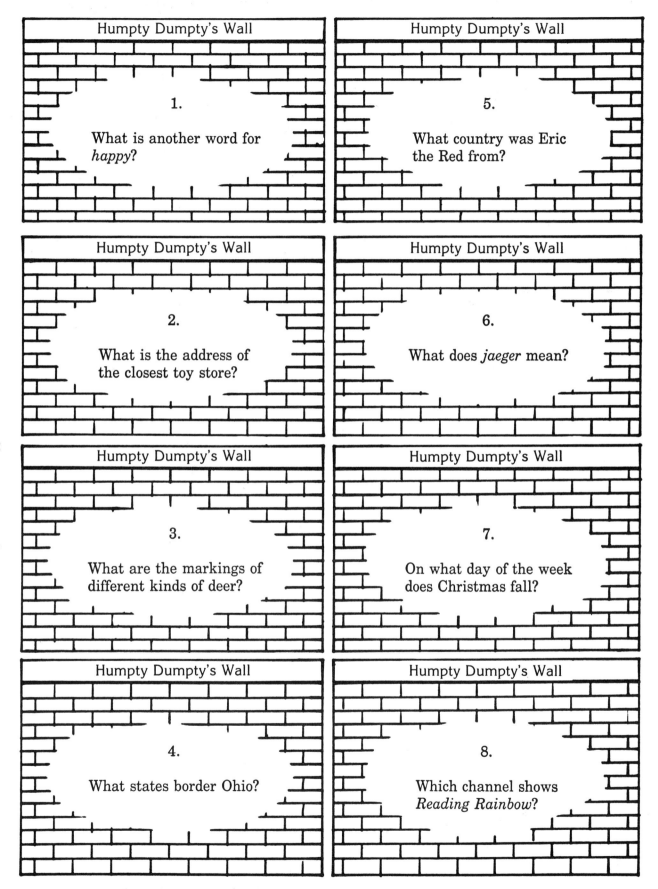

Humpty Dumpty's Wall

1.

What is another word for *happy*?

Humpty Dumpty's Wall

5.

What country was Eric the Red from?

Humpty Dumpty's Wall

2.

What is the address of the closest toy store?

Humpty Dumpty's Wall

6.

What does *jaeger* mean?

Humpty Dumpty's Wall

3.

What are the markings of different kinds of deer?

Humpty Dumpty's Wall

7.

On what day of the week does Christmas fall?

Humpty Dumpty's Wall

4.

What states border Ohio?

Humpty Dumpty's Wall

8.

Which channel shows *Reading Rainbow*?

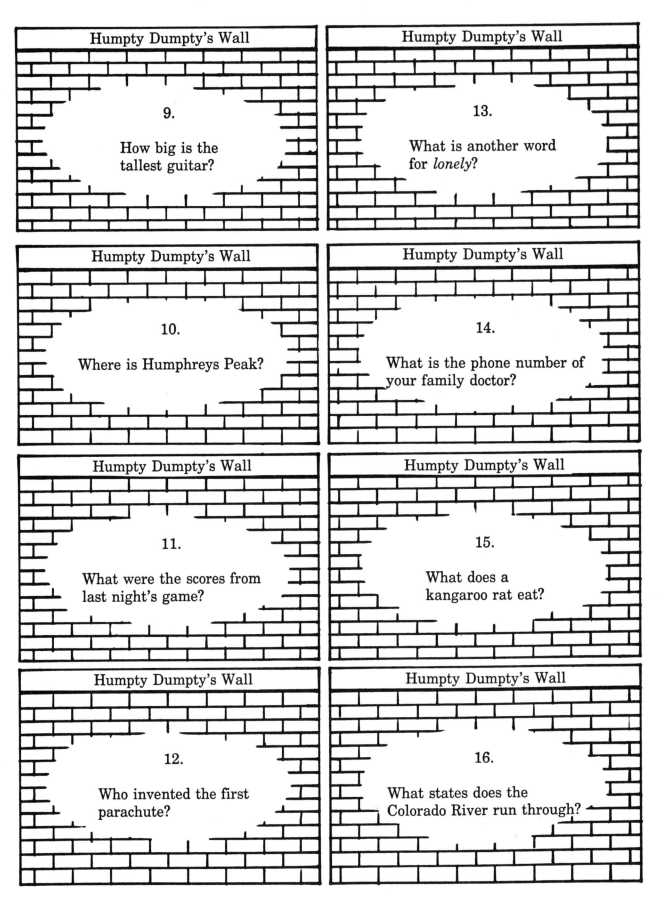

Humpty Dumpty's Wall

9.

How big is the
tallest guitar?

Humpty Dumpty's Wall

13.

What is another word
for *lonely*?

Humpty Dumpty's Wall

10.

Where is Humphreys Peak?

Humpty Dumpty's Wall

14.

What is the phone number of
your family doctor?

Humpty Dumpty's Wall

11.

What were the scores from
last night's game?

Humpty Dumpty's Wall

15.

What does a
kangaroo rat eat?

Humpty Dumpty's Wall

12.

Who invented the first
parachute?

Humpty Dumpty's Wall

16.

What states does the
Colorado River run through?

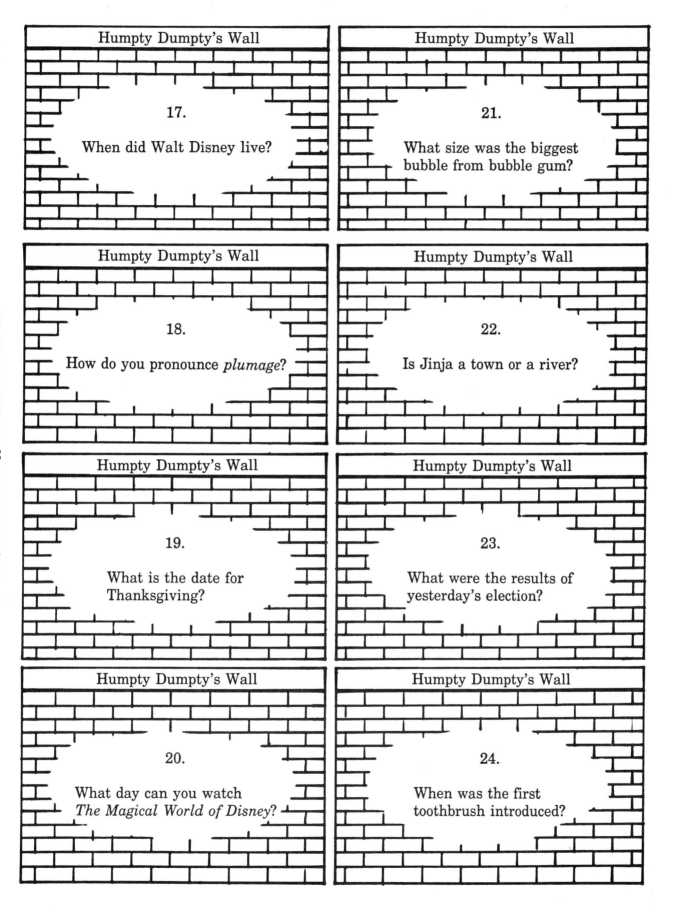

Humpty Dumpty's Wall

17.

When did Walt Disney live?

Humpty Dumpty's Wall

21.

What size was the biggest bubble from bubble gum?

Humpty Dumpty's Wall

18.

How do you pronounce *plumage*?

Humpty Dumpty's Wall

22.

Is Jinja a town or a river?

Humpty Dumpty's Wall

19.

What is the date for Thanksgiving?

Humpty Dumpty's Wall

23.

What were the results of yesterday's election?

Humpty Dumpty's Wall

20.

What day can you watch *The Magical World of Disney*?

Humpty Dumpty's Wall

24.

When was the first toothbrush introduced?

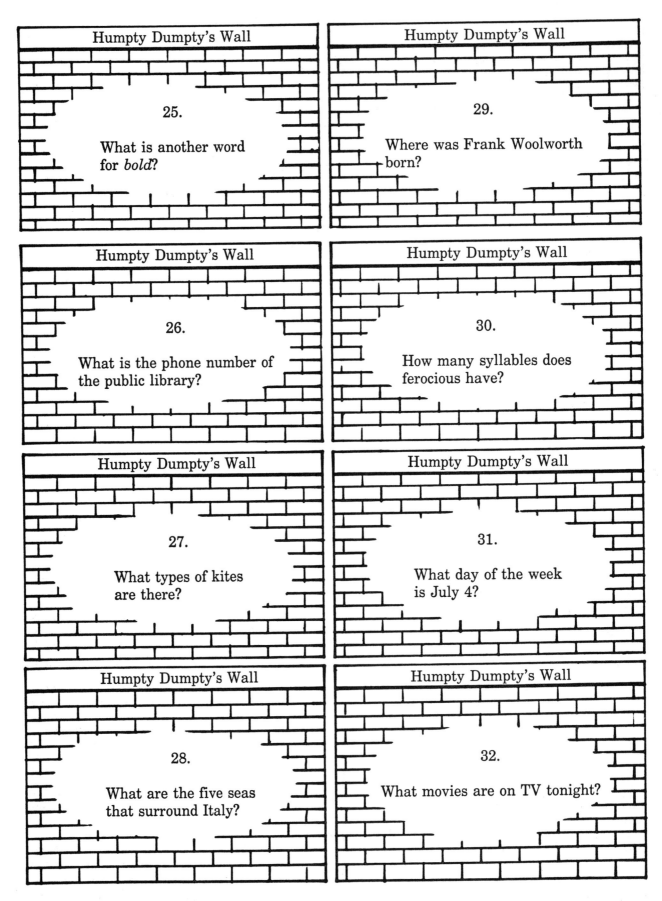

Humpty Dumpty's Wall

25.

What is another word for *bold*?

Humpty Dumpty's Wall

29.

Where was Frank Woolworth born?

Humpty Dumpty's Wall

26.

What is the phone number of the public library?

Humpty Dumpty's Wall

30.

How many syllables does ferocious have?

Humpty Dumpty's Wall

27.

What types of kites are there?

Humpty Dumpty's Wall

31.

What day of the week is July 4?

Humpty Dumpty's Wall

28.

What are the five seas that surround Italy?

Humpty Dumpty's Wall

32.

What movies are on TV tonight?

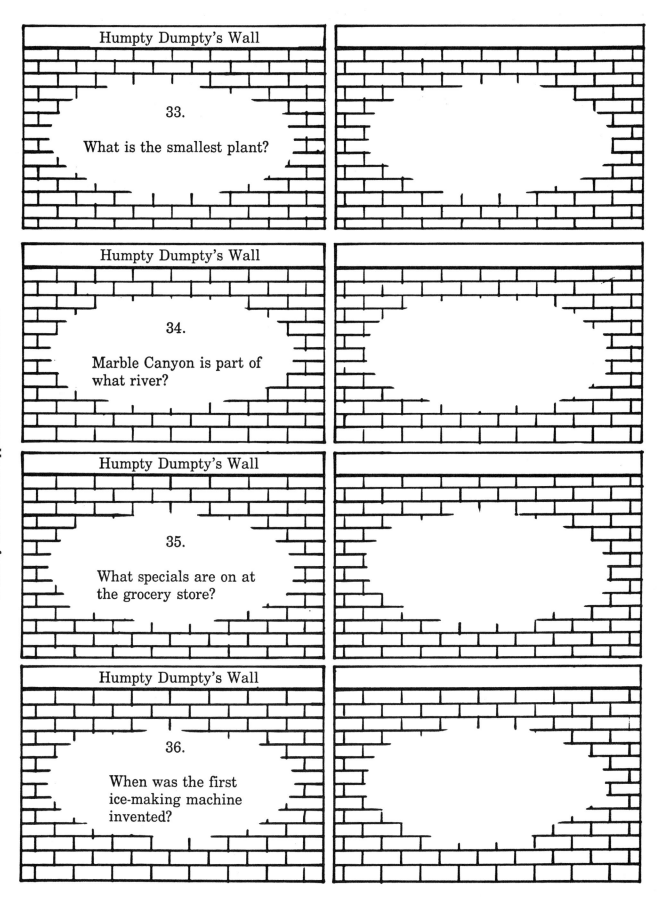

Humpty Dumpty's Wall

33.

What is the smallest plant?

Humpty Dumpty's Wall

34.

Marble Canyon is part of
what river?

Humpty Dumpty's Wall

35.

What specials are on at
the grocery store?

Humpty Dumpty's Wall

36.

When was the first
ice-making machine
invented?

WHO'S GOT THE ANSWER?

Skill Reinforced

Associating general (and a few specific) types of reference books with the kinds of information each contains

Associating the terms representing the parts of reference works with their definitions

Type of Activity

Whole class game

Grade Level: 4+

Time Required

One session

Prerequisites

PUT HUMPTY DUMPTY TOGETHER EGGS–ACTLY!

Introduction to reference terms (chronological order, entry words, headings, and so forth)

Materials

Who's Got the Answer game cards

Procedure

1. Distribute Who's Got the Answer game cards to the students (some may have two).
2. Select one student to stand and read the clue (question) on the bottom of his card.
3. The student who has the correct answer on his card stands and reads the answer. He then reads the next clue which is at the bottom of his card.
4. This continues until the beginning student stands again, this time with an answer.
5. Collect the cards, redistribute, and play again.

Variation

Make more game cards, adding more reference terms and more reference titles.

Follow-up Activities

REFERENCE RACE

practice using reference books

Who's Got the Answer?

answer:

calendar

next clue:

What is the alphabetical list of subjects found in the back of a book called?

Who's Got the Answer?

answer:

dictionary

next clue:

Which reference source has information on all subjects?

Who's Got the Answer?

answer:

index

next clue:

What is the page called that lists the chapters in a book?

Who's Got the Answer?

answer:

encyclopedia

next clue:

What source lists all the resources in the library media center?

Who's Got the Answer?

answer:

table of contents

next clue:

Which book lists synonyms?

Who's Got the Answer?

answer:

card catalog

next clue:

Which reference work is about people?

Who's Got the Answer?

answer:

thesaurus

next clue:

Which book contains words and their definitions?

Who's Got the Answer?

answer:

biographical dictionary

next clue:

Which book is an index to magazine articles?

Who's Got the Answer?

answer:

Readers' Guide

next clue:

What kind of publication comes out with a new issue every month or week?

Who's Got the Answer?

answer:

geographical dictionary

next clue:

Which book contains mostly maps?

Who's Got the Answer?

answer:

magazine

next clue:

Which encyclopedia tells about games like lacrosse, baseball, and hockey?

Who's Got the Answer?

answer:

atlas

next clue:

What are the words that you look up in a reference book called?

Who's Got the Answer?

answer:

Encyclopedia of Sports

next clue:

Which encyclopedia tells about thunder and lightning?

Who's Got the Answer?

answer:

entry words

next clue:

Which words are usually in bold print?

Who's Got the Answer?

answer:

Encyclopedia of Science

next clue:

Which dictionary is about places?

Who's Got the Answer?

answer:

headings

next clue:

What are the words in a question you use to look up information?

© 1990 by The Center for Applied Research in Education

Who's Got the Answer?

answer:

key words

next clue:

What are the words called that are usually at the top of a dictionary page?

Who's Got the Answer?

answer:

newspaper

next clue:

When a list is in time order, what is it called?

Who's Got the Answer?

answer:

guide words

next clue:

What is the small dictionary in the back of the book called?

Who's Got the Answer?

answer:

chronological

next clue:

When a list is in ABC order, what is it called?

Who's Got the Answer?

answer:

glossary

next clue:

What do we call the cabinet that contains pamphlets and pictures?

Who's Got the Answer?

answer:

alphabetical

next clue:

Which book has facts current this year?

Who's Got the Answer?

answer:

vertical file

next clue:

What daily publication covers current events?

Who's Got the Answer?

answer:

almanac

next clue:

Which book tells when things were invented?

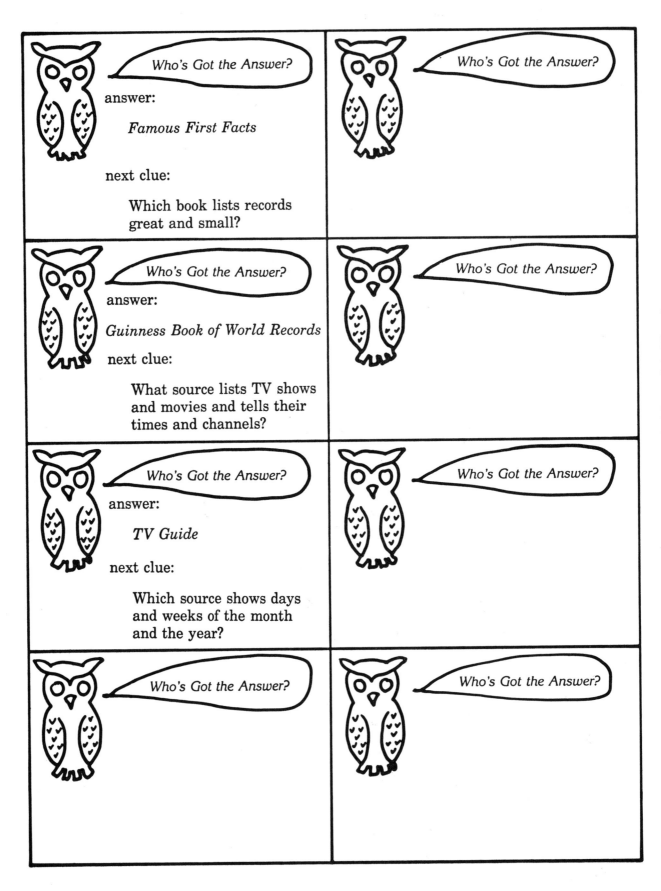

Who's Got the Answer?

answer:

Famous First Facts

next clue:

Which book lists records great and small?

Who's Got the Answer?

Who's Got the Answer?

answer:

Guinness Book of World Records

next clue:

What source lists TV shows and movies and tells their times and channels?

Who's Got the Answer?

Who's Got the Answer?

answer:

TV Guide

next clue:

Which source shows days and weeks of the month and the year?

Who's Got the Answer?

Who's Got the Answer?

Who's Got the Answer?

REFERENCE RACE

Skill Reinforced

Determining which reference book best answers a given question

Type of Activity

Whole class game

Grade Level: 5–6

Time Required

One session

Prerequisites

Introduction to reference books
HUMPTY DUMPTY'S WALL (part of PUT HUMPTY DUMPTY TOGETHER EGGS-ACTLY!)

Materials

Reference List
Reference Race answer sheets, reproduced for each student
Reference Race game cards
Clock or timer
Pencils

Procedure

1. Post the reference list so all students can see it; or, make a transparency and show it on the overhead projector.
2. Distribute one game card face down to each student. The rest of the cards should be placed so they are easily accessible to all students.
3. At the signal "GO," students read the question or statement on their cards and determine the reference source needed to find the answer.
4. Students write the reference source on their answer sheet next to the corresponding number, for example, the source for question 5 is written on line 5.
5. As students complete one card, they trade with another student for new cards or they exchange cards for one in the common stack.
6. Allow five to ten minutes for writing and trading. At the end of this time, give the correct answers so students can check their work.
7. The student with the most correct answers is the winner.

Variation

Add other questions and reference books.

Follow-up Activity

Have students look up answers to the questions in the appropriate reference books.

REFERENCE LIST:

ALMANAC

ENCYCLOPEDIA

BIOGRAPHICAL DICTIONARY

THESAURUS

GEOGRAPHICAL DICTIONARY

ATLAS

PERIODICAL GUIDE

DICTIONARY

QUOTATION BOOK

1.

What time did the sun rise on Jan. 1, 1981?

Reference Race!

2.

I want to learn about the Revolutionary War.

Reference Race!

3.

Why was Janet Scudder famous?

Reference Race!

4.

How can I get from New York City to Chicago?

Reference Race!

5.

In what state is Callaway County?

Reference Race!

6.

Where can I find a magazine article about dolphins?

Reference Race!

7.

What does *sovereignty* mean?

Reference Race!

8.

What is a synonym for *great*?

Reference Race!

9.

Where are the major cities of Australia located?

Reference Race!

10.

Where is Mount Saint Helens located?

Reference Race!

11.

Who was George Davenport?

Reference Race!

12.

Are there any magazine articles about television?

Reference Race!

13.

What are some of the colleges in Portland, Oregon?

Reference Race!

14.

Where can I learn about the Aztecs?

Reference Race!

15.

I need a map showing the products of Japan.

Reference Race!

16.

How much money does the President of the United States earn?

Reference Race!

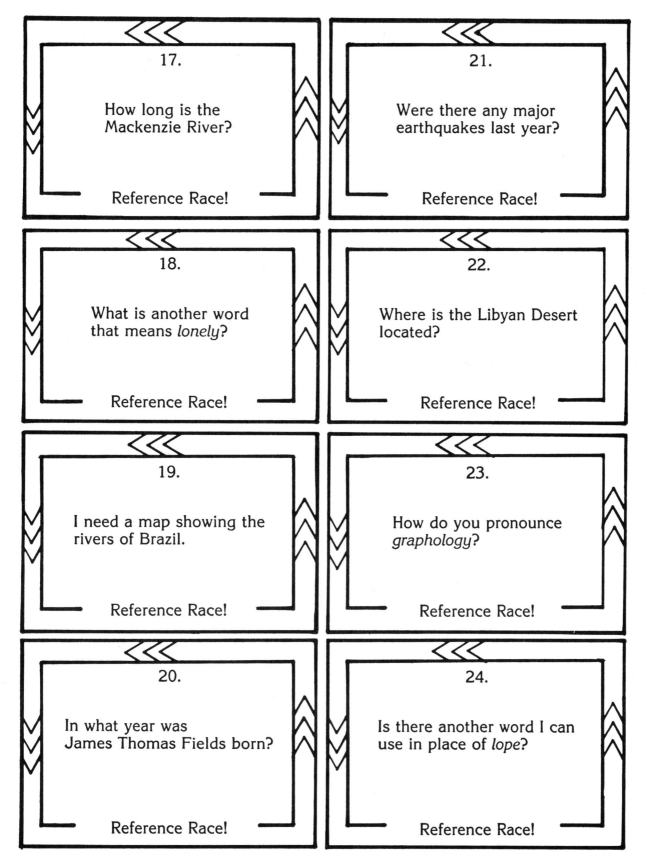

17.

How long is the
Mackenzie River?

Reference Race!

21.

Were there any major
earthquakes last year?

Reference Race!

18.

What is another word
that means *lonely*?

Reference Race!

22.

Where is the Libyan Desert
located?

Reference Race!

19.

I need a map showing the
rivers of Brazil.

Reference Race!

23.

How do you pronounce
graphology?

Reference Race!

20.

In what year was
James Thomas Fields born?

Reference Race!

24.

Is there another word I can
use in place of *lope*?

Reference Race!

25.

What part of speech is the word *quoin*?

Reference Race!

26.

In what year did Florence Nightingale die?

Reference Race!

27.

What countries border France?

Reference Race!

28.

What was the hottest day of the year in Phoenix, Arizona?

Reference Race!

29.

Who is the senior senator from Arizona?

Reference Race!

30.

Where was William Mitchell born?

Reference Race!

31.

What is the climate of Peru like?

Reference Race!

32.

Are there any magazine articles about Egypt?

Reference Race!

33.

Who said the famous line: "Give me liberty or give me death"?

Reference Race!

34.

What is the address of the American Medical Association?

Reference Race!

35.

What is another word for *hungry*?

Reference Race!

36.

Who said, "Nothing succeeds like success"?

Reference Race!

Reference Race Answers:

1. almanac
2. encyclopedia
3. biographical dictionary
4. atlas
5. geographical dictionary
6. periodical guide
7. dictionary
8. thesaurus
9. atlas
10. geographical dictionary or atlas
11. biographical dictionary
12. periodical guide
13. geographical dictionary
14. encyclopedia
15. atlas
16. almanac
17. geographical dictionary
18. thesaurus
19. atlas
20. biographical dictionary
21. almanac
22. geographical dictionary
23. dictionary
24. thesaurus
25. dictionary
26. biographical dictionary
27. atlas
28. almanac
29. almanac
30. biographical dictionary
31. encyclopedia
32. periodical guide
33. quotation book
34. almanac
35. thesaurus
36. quotation book

Name _____

REFERENCE RACE ANSWER SHEET
1. _____
2. _____
3. _____
4. _____
5. _____
6. _____
7. _____
8. _____
9. _____
10. _____
11. _____
12. _____
13. _____
14. _____
15. _____
16. _____
17. _____
18. _____
19. _____
20. _____
21. _____
22. _____
23. _____
24. _____
25. _____
26. _____
27. _____
28. _____
29. _____
30. _____
31. _____
32. _____
33. _____
34. _____
35. _____
36. _____

Name _____

REFERENCE RACE ANSWER SHEET
1. _____
2. _____
3. _____
4. _____
5. _____
6. _____
7. _____
8. _____
9. _____
10. _____
11. _____
12. _____
13. _____
14. _____
15. _____
16. _____
17. _____
18. _____
19. _____
20. _____
21. _____
22. _____
23. _____
24. _____
25. _____
26. _____
27. _____
28. _____
29. _____
30. _____
31. _____
32. _____
33. _____
34. _____
35. _____
36. _____

CHOOSE AND CHECK

Skill Reinforced

Practicing basic skills

Type of Activity

Individual or partner
Center

Grade Level: 2–6

Time Required

One session as follow-up for each prerequisite lesson

Prerequisites

Lesson Subject	Follow-up Activities
fiction order	Fiction Call Numbers (football)
nonfiction order	Nonfiction Call Numbers (football)
guide words	Before, After, or On That Page! (butterfly)
encyclopedias	Am I in This Volume? (butterfly)
card catalog	Catalog Cards (duck)
Children's Magazine Guide	Periodical Entries (duck)

Materials

Pencil
Desired shapes (reproduce and cut out, punch holes, and write correct answers on the backs, according to the answer pages that follow shapes. It's best to laminate.)

Procedure

1. A student picks up a shape so the front faces her.
2. She chooses a hole and puts the pencil tip into it.
3. She gives the answer and turns the shape over to check whether the answer is correct.
4. The student picks another shape and continues until she has practiced with all of them.

Variations

- This can be played with partners. One player is the teacher/leader and holds the shape so the other player sees the front. The player puts a pencil tip into a hole and gives the answer. If the answer is correct, a point is scored and the student continues practicing. The partners take turns being the teacher/leader. The winner is the player who scores the most points.
- Additional skills that could be practiced using this same format are using an index, using a table of contents, and reading bibliographic information.

Choose and Check: Fiction

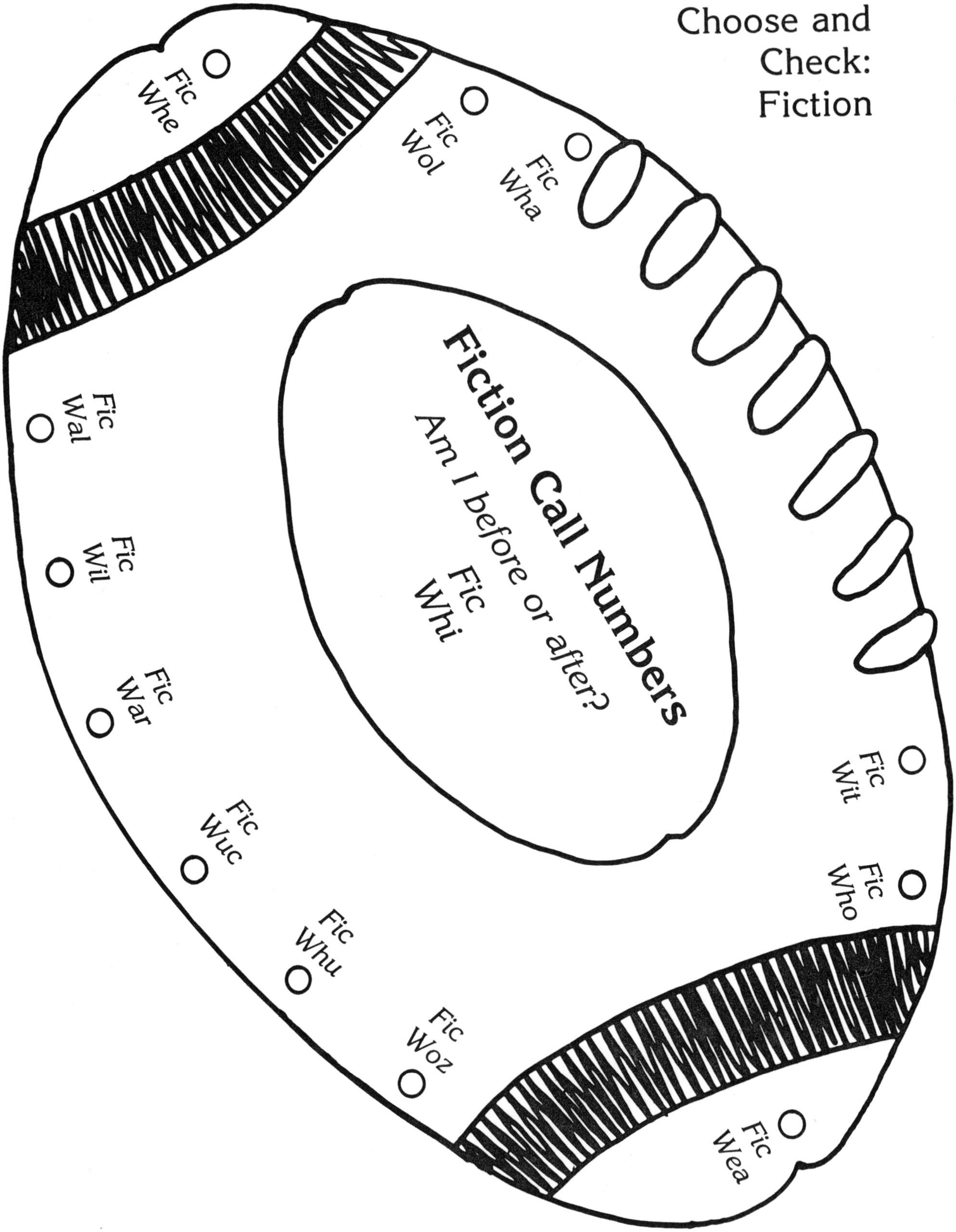

Fiction Call Numbers
Am I before or after?
Fic Whi
Fic Whe
Fic Wol
Fic Wha
Fic Wal
Fic Wil
Fic War
Fic Wuc
Fic Whu
Fic Woz
Fic Wea
Fic Who
Fic Wit

Choose and
Check:
Fiction

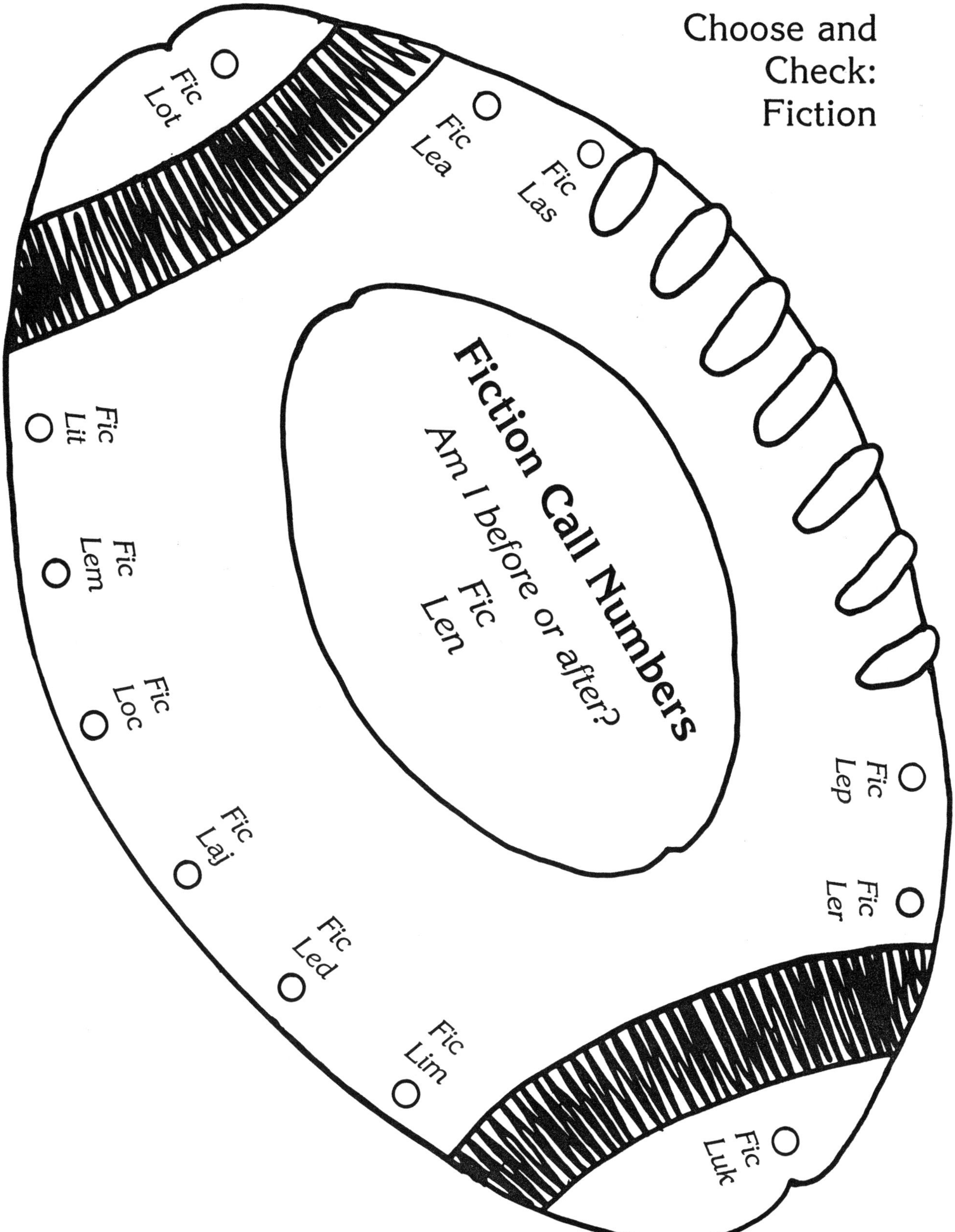

Fic
Lot ○

Fic
Lea ○

Fic
Las ○

Fiction Call Numbers

Am I before or after?

Fic
Len

Fic
Lit ○

Fic
Lem ○

Fic
Loc ○

Fic
Laj ○

Fic
Led ○

Fic
Lim ○

Fic
Lep ○

Fic
Ler ○

Fic
Luk ○

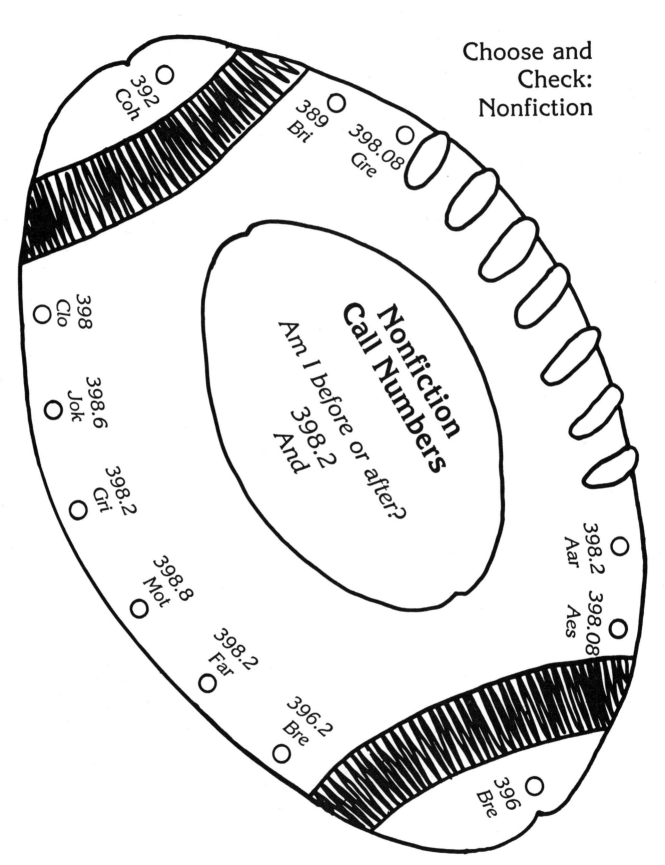

Choose and Check: Nonfiction

Nonfiction Call Numbers

Am I before or after? 398.2 And

392 Coh

389 Bri

398.08 Gre

398 Clo

398.6 Jok

398.2 Gri

398.8 Mot

398.2 Far

396.2 Bre

396 Bre

398.2 Aar

398.08 Aes

Choose and Check: Nonfiction

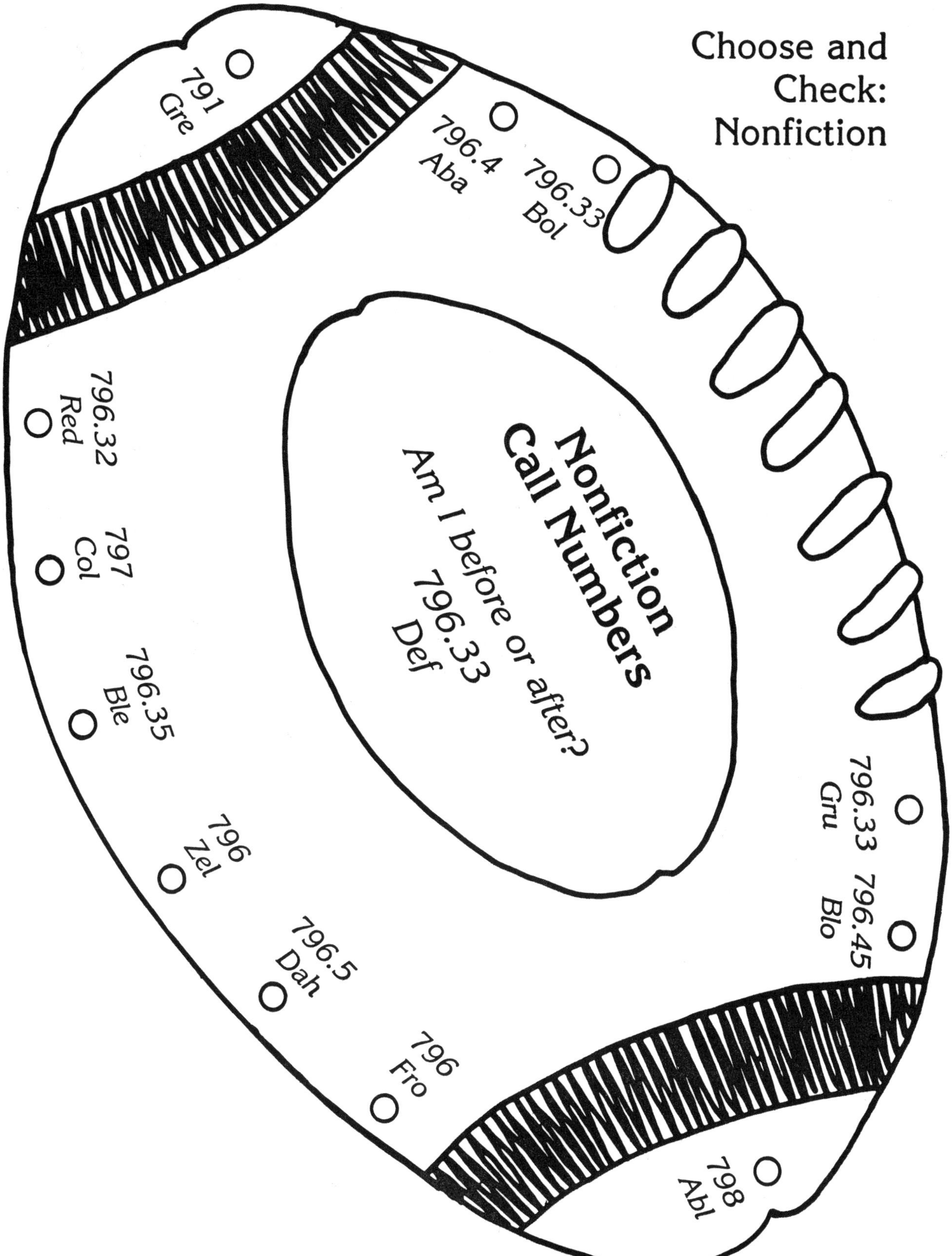

Nonfiction Call Numbers
Am I before or after?
796.33
Def
791
Gre
796.4
Aba
796.33
Bol
796.32
Red
797
Col
796.35
Ble
796
Zel
796.5
Dah
796
Fro
798
Abl
796.33
Gru
796.45
Blo

Answers A = after; B = before (answer position as seen from front)

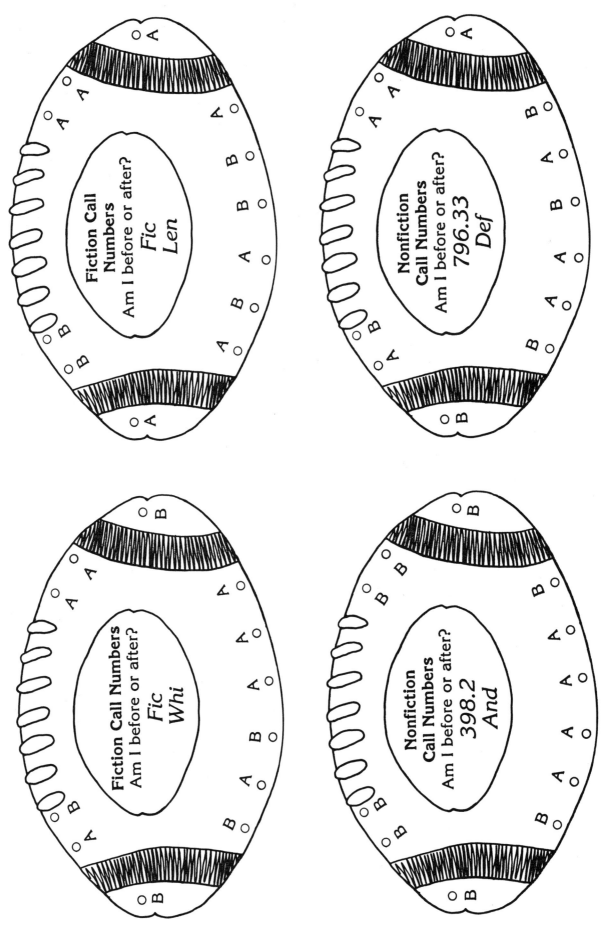

Fiction Call Numbers
Am I before or after?
Fic
Len

Fiction Call Numbers
Am I before or after?
Fic
Whi

Nonfiction Call Numbers
Am I before or after?
796.33
Def

Nonfiction Call Numbers
Am I before or after?
398.2
And

Choose and Check: Guide Words

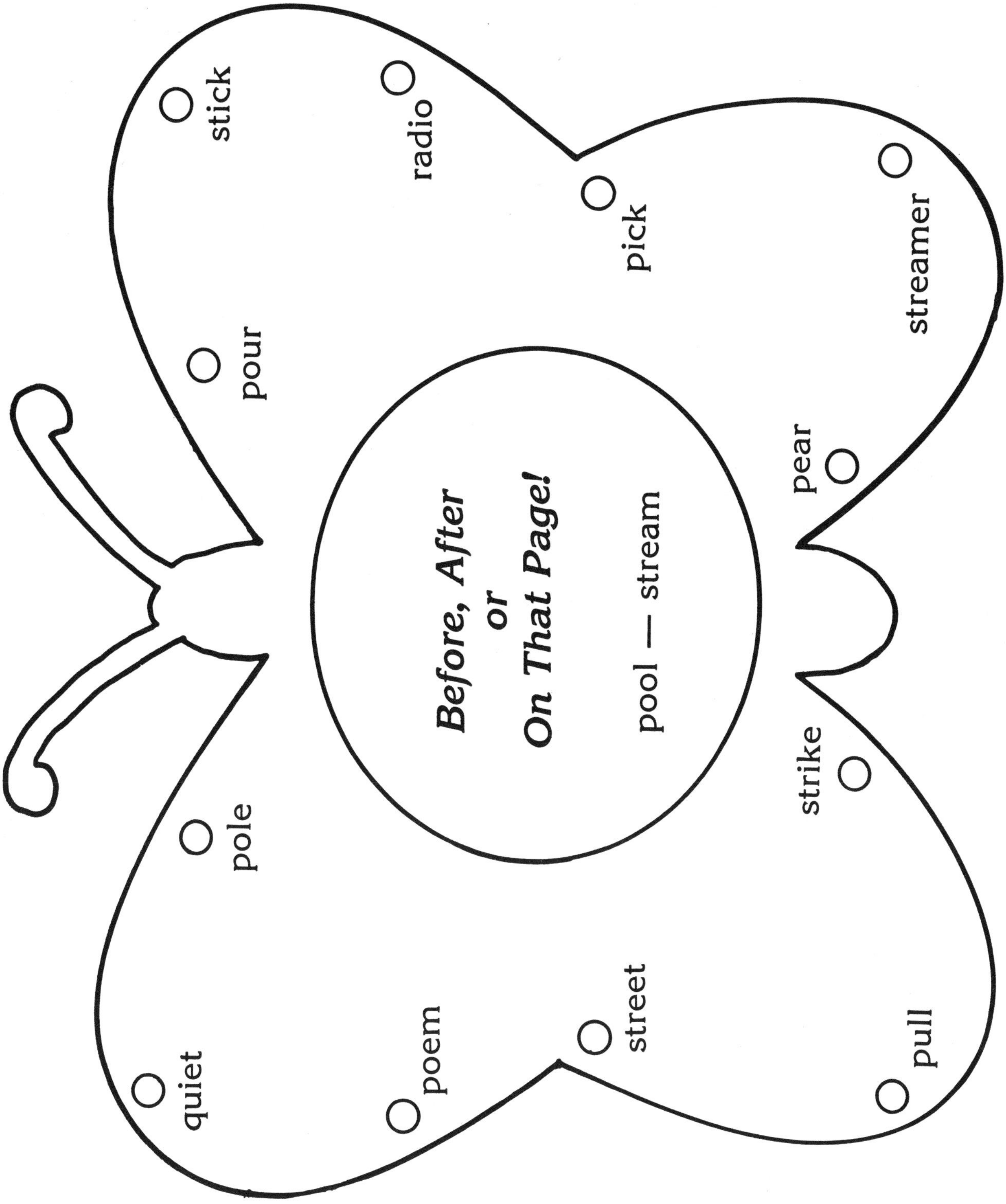
Before, After
or
On That Page!
pool — stream
stick
radio
pick
streamer
pour
pear
strike
pole
quiet
poem
street
pull

Choose and Check: Guide Words

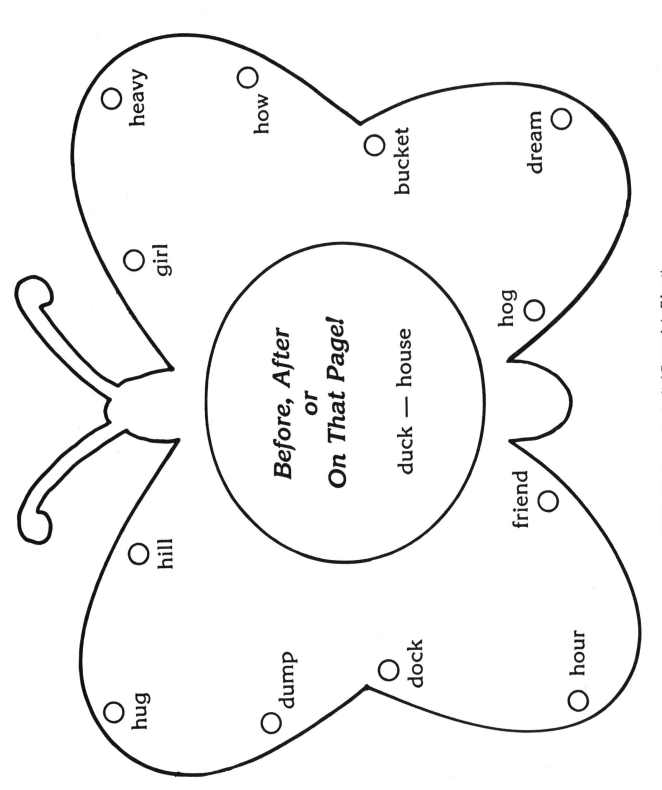

heavy

how

bucket

dream

girl

hog

Before, After
or
On That Page!

duck — house

hill

friend

hug

dump

dock

hour

Choose and Check: Volumes

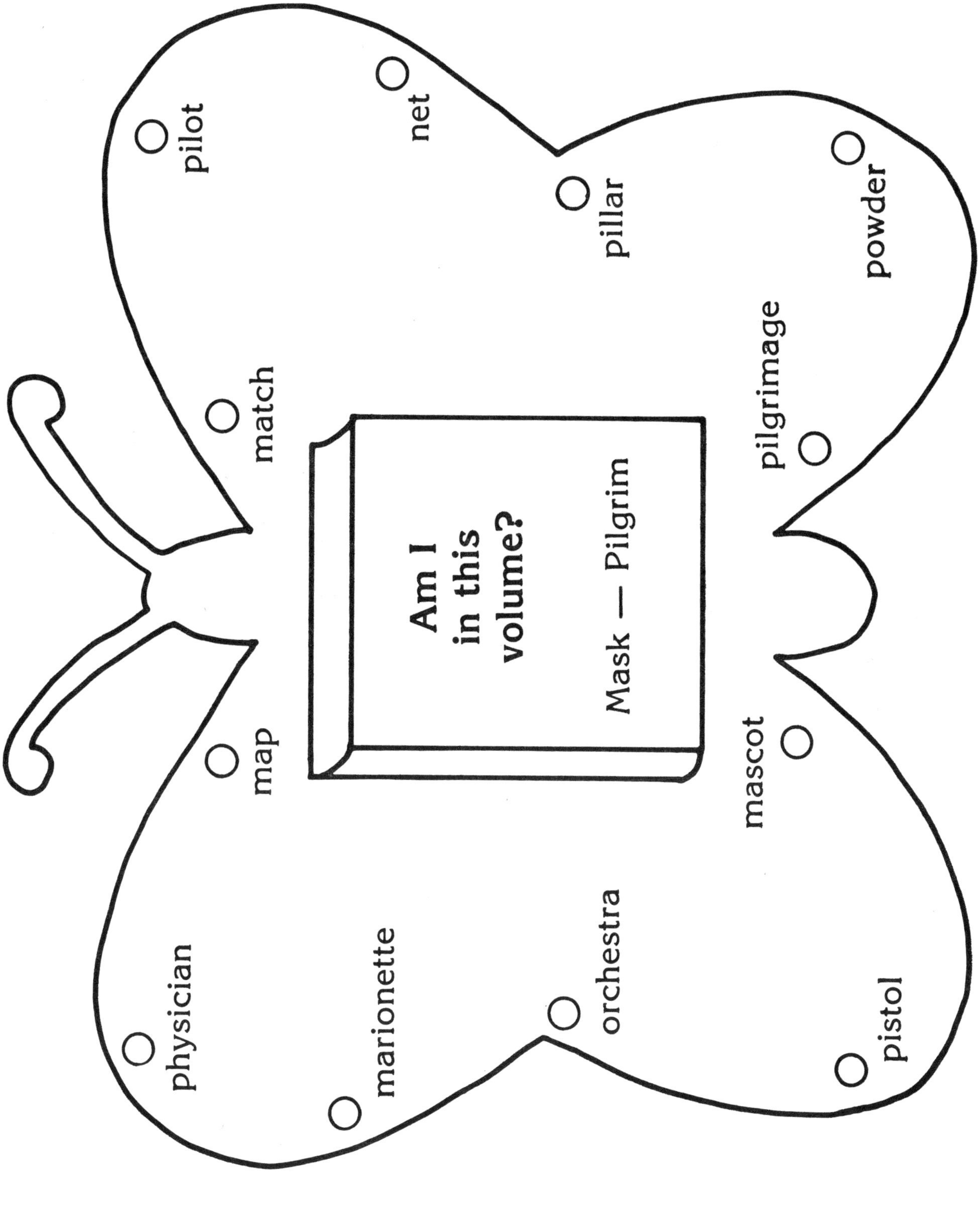

Am I
in this
volume?
Mask — Pilgrim
pilot
net
pillar
powder
match
pilgrimage
map
mascot
physician
marionette
orchestra
pistol

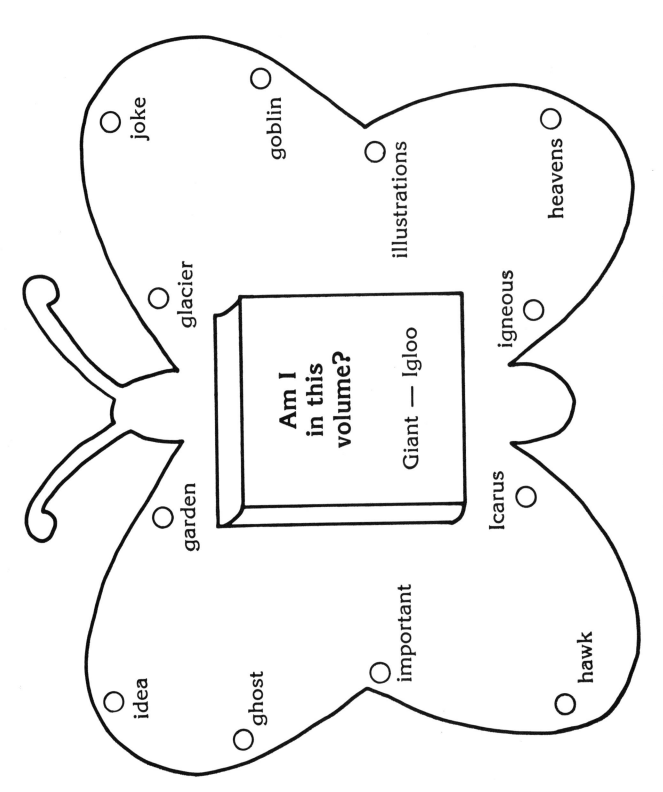

joke

goblin

illustrations

heavens

glacier

igneous

Am I
in this
volume?

Giant — Igloo

garden

Icarus

important

idea

ghost

hawk

Answers A = after; B = before; N = no; Y = yes

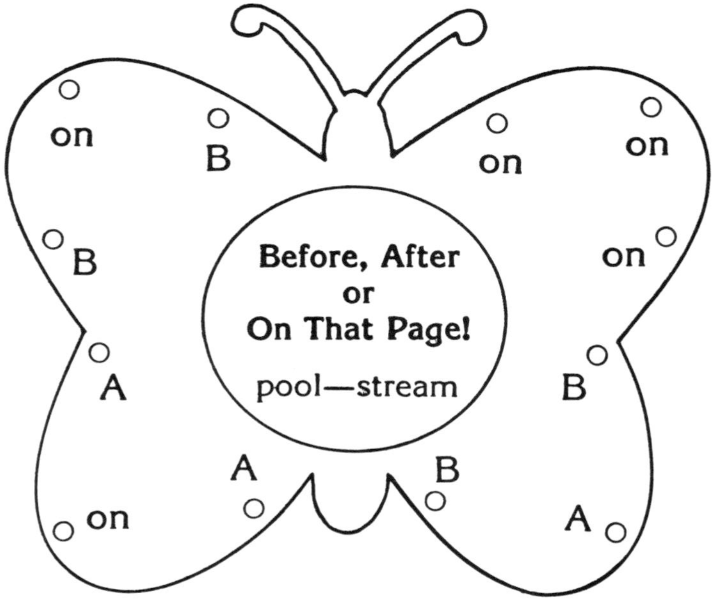

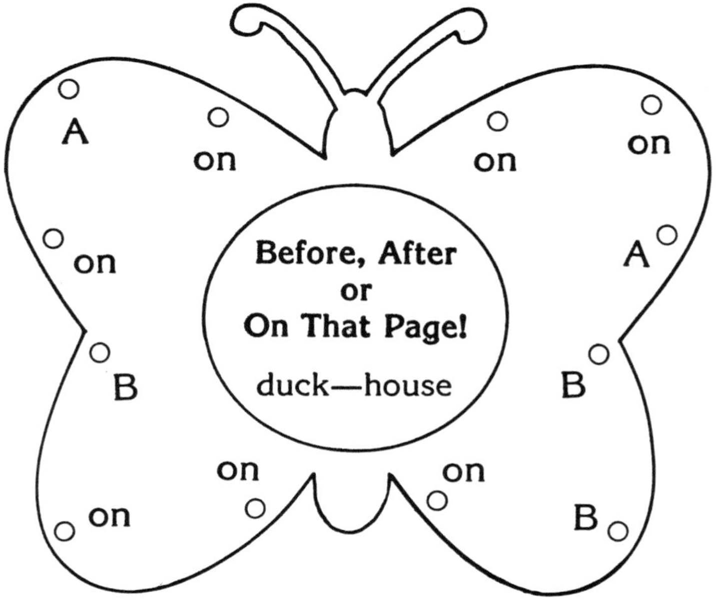

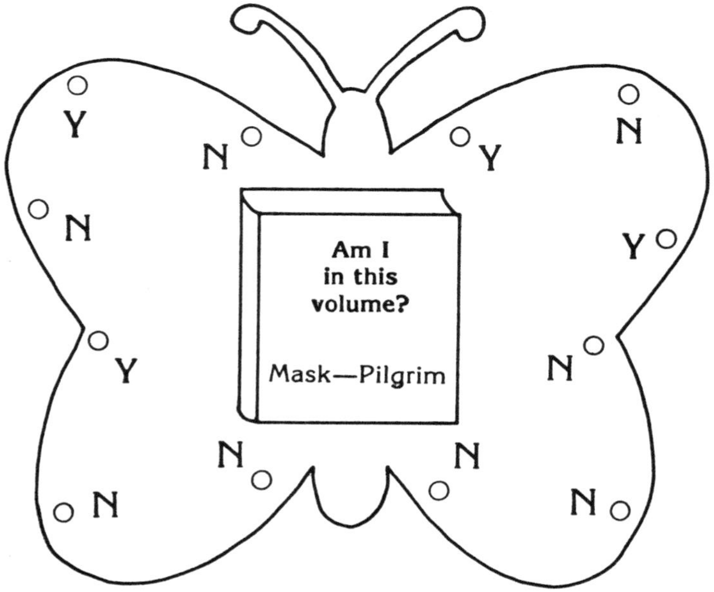

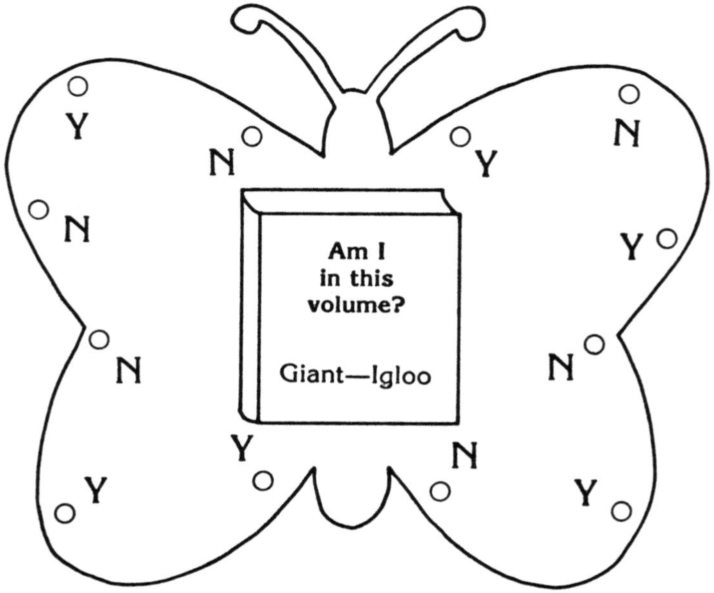

Before, After or On That Page!
pool—stream

B
A
on
on
on
B
A
on
B
A
on

Before, After or On That Page!
duck—house

on
A
B
B
on
on
on
A
B
on

Am I in this volume?
Mask—Pilgrim

N
Y
N
Y
N
N
N
Y
N
Y
N
N

Am I in this volume?
Giant—Igloo

N
Y
N
Y
Y
N
N
Y
N
Y
N
Y

Choose and Check: Catalog Cards

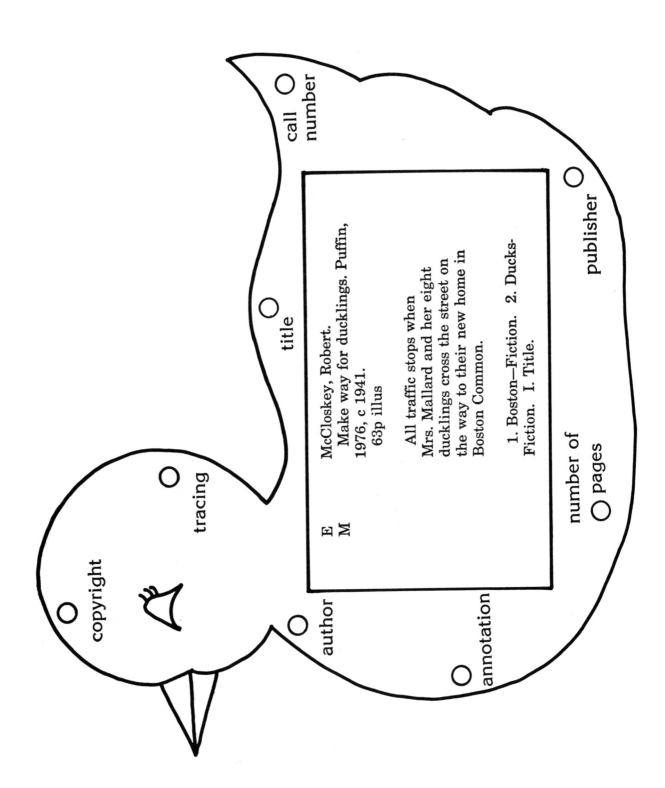

call number

publisher

title

number of pages

tracing

copyright

author

annotation

McCloskey, Robert.
Make way for ducklings. Puffin, 1976, c 1941.
63p illus

All traffic stops when Mrs. Mallard and her eight ducklings cross the street on the way to their new home in Boston Common.

1. Boston—Fiction. 2. Ducks-Fiction. I. Title.

E
M

Choose and Check: Catalog Cards

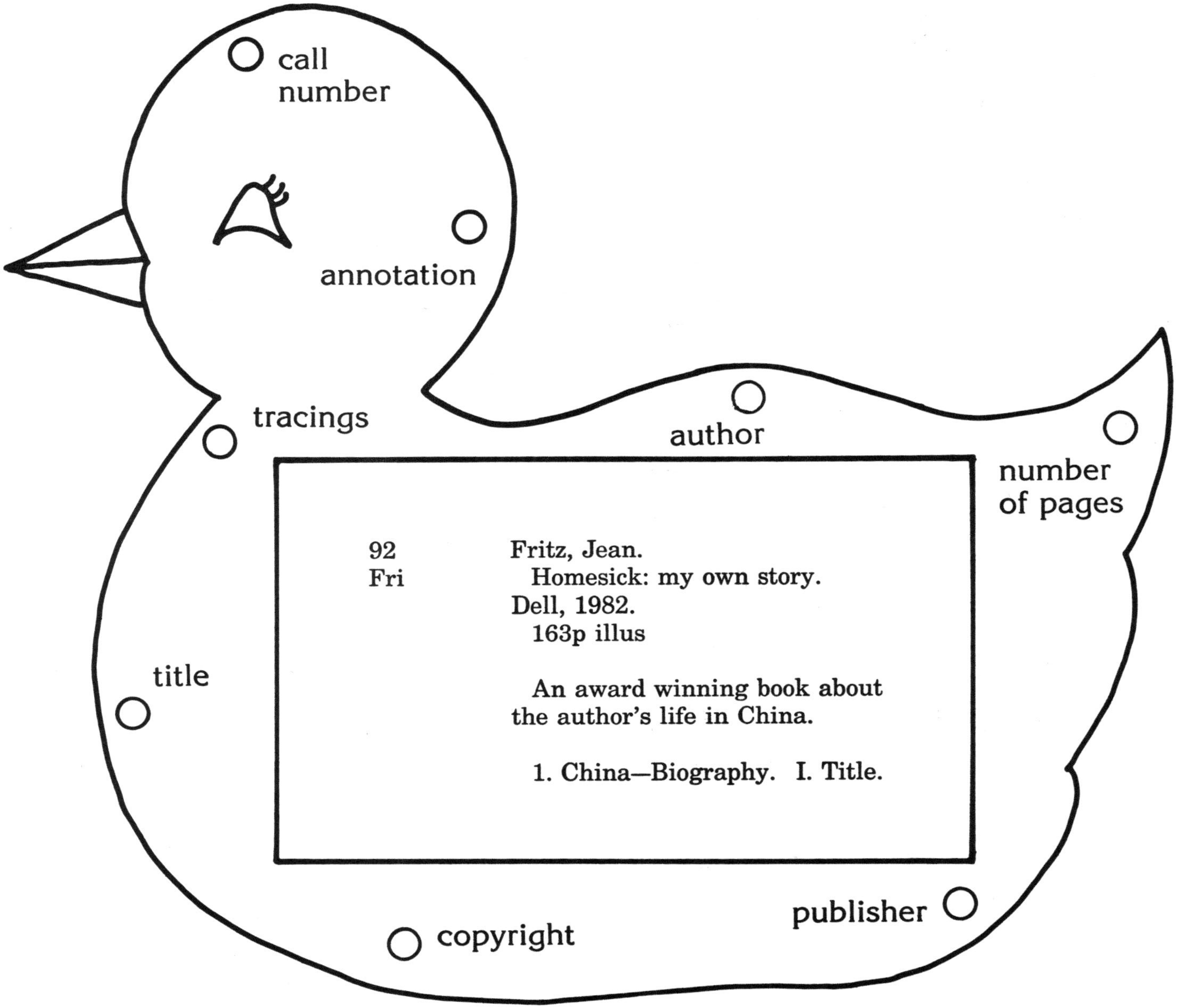

number of pages

publisher

author

copyright

call number

annotation

tracings

title

Fritz, Jean.
  Homesick: my own story.
Dell, 1982.
163p illus

  An award winning book about
the author's life in China.

  1. China—Biography. I. Title.

92
Fri

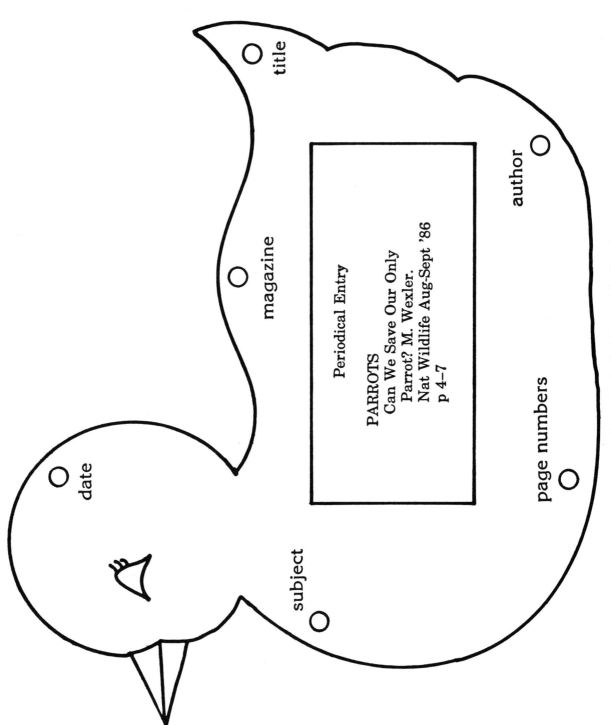

title

author

magazine

Periodical Entry

PARROTS
Can We Save Our Only
Parrot? M. Wexler.
Nat Wildlife Aug-Sept '86
p 4–7

page numbers

date

subject

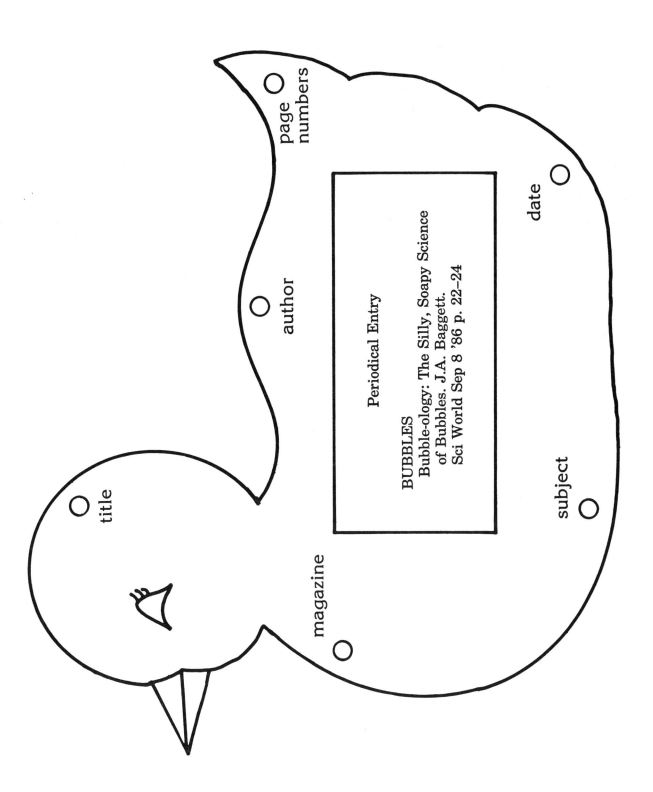

page
numbers

date

author

title

magazine

subject

Periodical Entry

BUBBLES
Bubble-ology: The Silly, Soapy Science
of Bubbles. J.A. Baggett.
Sci World Sep 8 '86 p. 22–24

Answers

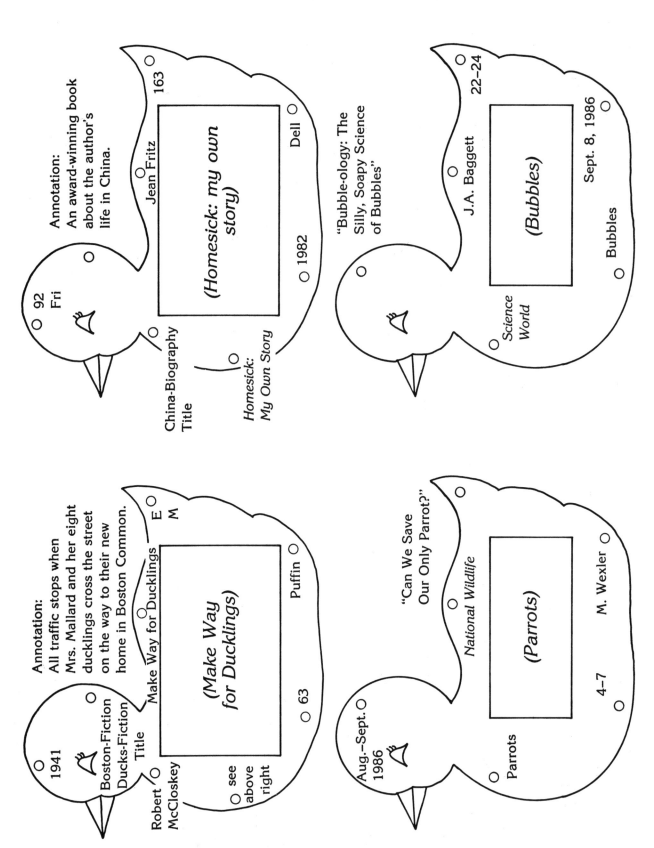

Annotation:
An award-winning book about the author's life in China.

92
Fri

China-Biography
Title

Jean Fritz

(Homesick: my own story)

Homesick: My Own Story

1982

Dell

163

"Bubble-ology: The Silly, Soapy Science of Bubbles"

J.A. Baggett

22–24

(Bubbles)

Sept. 8, 1986

Science World

Bubbles

Annotation:
All traffic stops when Mrs. Mallard and her eight ducklings cross the street on the way to their new home in Boston Common.

1941

Boston-Fiction
Ducks-Fiction
Title

Robert McCloskey

Make Way for Ducklings

(Make Way for Ducklings)

see above right

63

Puffin

E
M

"Can We Save Our Only Parrot?"

National Wildlife

Aug.–Sept. 1986

Parrots

(Parrots)

4–7

M. Wexler

MOTHER GOOSE BOOK

Skill Reinforced

Introducing concepts of table of contents and index

Type of Activity

Whole class art

Grade Level: 1–3

Time Required

One or two sessions for coloring pages (Procedures 1–4); one session for teaching concepts (Procedures 5–10)

Prerequisite

Knowledge of nursery rhymes contained in the *Mother Goose Book* on the following pages

Materials

Mother Goose Book, reproduced front to back, folded, and stapled
Crayons
Pencils
Transparency of table of contents and index pages
Transparency marker

Procedure

1. Review nursery rhymes with students.
2. If students can read, they may proceed directly to drawing and coloring an appropriate picture on each page. As many first graders are just starting to read, the teacher/librarian must tell the students which rhyme is on each page, one or two pages at a time.
3. Students may draw a picture of Mother Goose on the cover and write their names as illustrators.
4. When all the pages have pictures, students will be able to identify which nursery rhyme is on each page and will be ready for the rest of the activity.
5. Using the table of contents part of the transparency, have students tell you which page each rhyme is on. Write the page number on the transparency. Students should record the answers in their books.
6. Do the same for the index.
7. With the table of contents and index transparencies side by side, ask students if they can tell what kind of order each is in. You may have to guide the youngest classes, but usually someone is able to pick it up.
8. Have students turn to the table of contents in their books. Ask them where it is— yes, it is in the front of the book.

9. Have students turn to the index—yes, it is in the back of the book.

10. Have students use the table of contents and index to locate specific nursery rhymes.

Follow-up Activity

NURSERY RHYME PUZZLES

Mother Goose
Book

Illustrated by

_____

TABLE OF CONTENTS

INDEX

Jack Be Nimble

Jack be nimble,
Jack be quick,
Jack jump over
The candlestick.

Mary Had a Little Lamb

Mary had a little lamb,
Its fleece was white as snow.
And everywhere that Mary went,
The lamb was sure to go.

Hey Diddle, Diddle

Hey diddle, diddle,
The cat and the fiddle,
The cow jumped over the moon;
The little dog laughed
To see such a sport,
And the dish ran away with the spoon.

Baa Baa Black Sheep

Baa Baa Black Sheep
Have you any wool?
Yes, sir, yes, sir,
Three bags full;
One for the master,
And one for the dame,
And one for the little boy
Who lives down the lane

Humpty Dumpty

Humpty Dumpty sat on a wall,
Humpty Dumpty had a great fall;
All the king's horses and all the king's men
Couldn't put Humpty together again.

Little Miss Muffet

Little Miss Muffet
Sat on a tuffet,
Eating her curds and whey,
There came a big spider,
Who sat down beside her,
And frightened Miss Muffet away.

Hickory, Dickory, Dock!

Hickory, dickory, dock!
The mouse ran up the clock;
The clock struck one,
The mouse ran down,
Hickory, dickory, dock.

Three Blind Mice

Three blind mice. Three blind mice.
See how they run. See how they run.
They all ran after the farmer's wife,
She cut off their tails with a carving knife.
Did you ever see such a thing in your life,
As three blind mice?

NURSERY RHYME PUZZLES

Skill Reinforced

Using an index

Type of Activity

Small group, partners, or individual
Center

Grade Level: 1–3

Time Required

One session

Prerequisite

Knowledge of nursery rhymes

Materials

Nursery rhyme pages reproduced onto card stock and cut into puzzle pieces
Two manila envelopes (9 by 6 inches) with reproduced instructions glued on
Several nursery rhyme books with indexes

Procedure

1. Place the pieces of two puzzles in each manila envelope.
2. Students using the center select an envelope and follow the instructions on it.

Instructions for Envelopes

NURSERY RHYME PUZZLES

1. Put the two puzzles together.
2. Decide which nursery rhyme is illustrated in each puzzle.
3. Use the index in a nursery rhyme book to look up each rhyme.
4. Read each rhyme aloud (softly).
5. Put the puzzle pieces back in the envelope.

Variations

- Make more puzzles by using pictures from nursery rhyme coloring books, or have students draw their own pictures. Mount the pictures on poster or tag board and cut into puzzle pieces. Place two puzzles with the same color of backing into one envelope and attach instructions.
- The puzzles can be easy or difficult depending on how many pieces each is cut into. Four to six pieces in each puzzle is plenty for first graders.

Nursery Rhyme Puzzles

Nursery Rhyme Puzzles

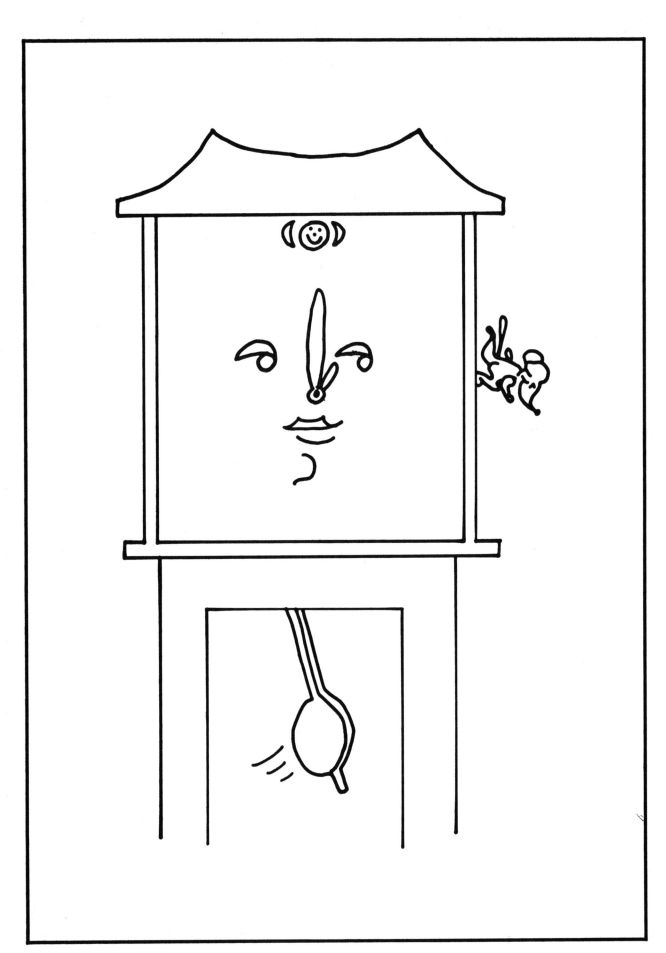

Nursery Rhyme Puzzles

Nursery Rhyme Puzzles

NATIONAL GEOGRAPHIC INDEX

Skill Reinforced

Using a periodic index

Type of Activity

Center

Grade Level: 4–6

Time Required

One or two sessions

Prerequisite

Introduction to the *National Geographic* and its index

Materials

Six file folders
Sample entry reproduced six times
Six sample pages reproduced
National Geographic Index Questions and Answers reproduced
Lined paper
Pencils

Preparation

1. Place a sample entry on the front of each file folder.
2. Place a sample page on the left inside of each file folder.
3. Place questions for that sample page on the right inside of the file folder.
4. Answers may be placed on the back of the file folder or kept by the teacher.
5. Laminate the file folders.

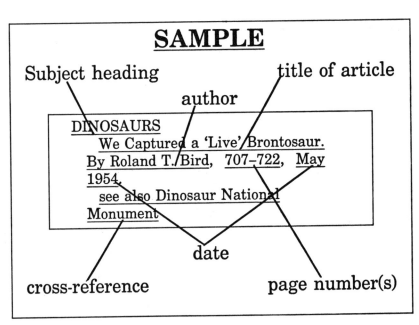

Procedure

1. Student selects one of the six file folders from the center.
2. Student makes her own answer sheet by numbering down the side of a sheet of lined paper.
3. Student uses the sample pages from the *National Geographic Index* to answer the questions in the file folder.
4. Student or teacher checks answers against the answer key.

Variation

Reproduce a few pages from *Reader's Guide* and write up questions for students to answer using those sample pages.

Follow-up Activities

Students can look up subjects they are interested in in the actual index. If the *National Geographic* issues referred to are available in the school LMC, they can be requested and used for research. If the issues are not available in the school, the student already has the information to help locate them at the public library. PERIODICAL ENTRIES (see CHOOSE AND CHECK)

Questions for page 200 of the National Geographic Index:

1. What is the title of the second article on battleships?
2. Which issue contains an article on bauxite?
3. What other phrase can be used for *battle monuments*?
4. On which pages would you expect to find the first article on battlefields?
5. Who is the author of the third article on Bavaria?

Questions for page 270 of the National Geographic Index:

1. What other subjects could you look up to find more information about airplane carriers?
2. Who is the author of the second article on carnivorous plants?
3. What is the title of the fourth article under *CARNIVAL*?
4. In which issue would you find the first article on the Caroline Islands?
5. On which pages are you likely to find photographs by Jeff Carter?

Questions for page 455 of the National Geographic Index:

1. Who wrote the article entitled "The Ghosts of Jericho"?
2. On which pages would you expect to find the second article on geysers?
3. What is the former name of Ghana?
4. Which issue has the most recent article on giant kelp?
5. What is the title of the third article about West Germany?

Questions for page 704 of the National Geographic Index:

1. What is the title of the last article about monkeys?
2. On which pages would you expect to find the second article on money?
3. What is another name for monitor lizards?
4. Who is the author of the fifth article on Mongolia?
5. In which issue would you find the first article on Mongols?

Questions for page 888 of the National Geographic Index:

1. What is the cross reference for roaches?
2. On which pages would you expect to find an article on Roan Mountain?
3. What is the title of the fourth article about Roanoke Island?
4. Who is the author of the article on Robert Frost?
5. In which issue would you find an article on roadrunners?

Questions for page 1042 of the National Geographic Index:

1. On which pages would you expect to find an article on the Tuscarora Indians?
2. Name two cross references for the subject of turtles.
3. Who is the author of the last article on Tutankhamun?
4. What is the title of the third article about Tuscany?
5. In which issue are you likely to find photographs by David Turnley?

THE NATIONAL GEOGRAPHIC INDEX

Answers for page 200:

1. "Midshipmen's Cruise"
2. August, 1978
3. War Memorials
4. 4–57
5. Fitzhugh Lee Minnigerode

Answers for page 270:

1. aircraft carriers, escort carriers
2. Paul A. Zahl
3. "Brazil, Oba!"
4. October, 1986
5. 230–257

Answers for page 455:

1. James L. Kelso
2. 109–130
3. Gold Coast
4. September, 1980
5. "The Danube: River of Many Nations"

Answers for page 704:

1. "Monkey Folk"
2. 745–768
3. Komodo Dragons
4. Owen Lattimore
5. November, 1982

Answers for page 888:

1. cockroaches
2. 819–828
3. "Indian Life Before the Colonists Came"
4. Archibald MacLeish
5. May, 1983

Answers for page 1042:

1. 375–403
2. green turtles, tortoises
3. Maynard Owen Williams
4. Leonardo da Vinci: A Man for All Ages
5. October, 1988

Sample Page

BATTAGLIA, LEE E.

Photos by Bruce Dale. 615-637, *May 1973*
How Bats Hunt With Sound. By J.J.G. McCue. 571-578, *Apr. 1961*
Mystery Mammals of the Twilight. By Donald R. Griffin. 117-134, *July 1946*
Bats of the Carlsbad Cavern (New Mexico). By Vernon Bailey. 321-330, *Sept. 1925*
A Mexican Land of Canaan: Marvelous Riches of the Wonderful West Coast of Our Neighbor Republic. By Frederick Simpich. 307-330, *Oct. 1919*
Nature's Transformation at Panama: The Remarkable Changes in Faunal and Physical Conditions in the Gatun Lake Region. By George Shiras, 3d. 159-194, *Aug. 1915*

BATTAGLIA, LEE E.:
Nomination Page. *Oct. 1963*
Author-Photographer
Wedding of Two Worlds (Sikkim). 708-727, *Nov. 1963*
Photographer
History Revealed in Ancient Glass. By Ray Winfield Smith. Photos by B. Anthony Stewart and Lee E. Battaglia. 346-369, *Sept. 1964*
Last Moments of the Pompeians. By Amedeo Maiuri. Paintings by Peter V. Bianchi. 651-669, *Nov. 1961*

BATTLE For a Bigger Bob. By Mike Edwards. Photos by Dewitt Jones. 690-692, *May 1985*

BATTLE GLACIER, British Columbia, Canada:
Some Tramps Across the Glaciers and Snowfields of British Columbia. By Howard Palmer. 457-487, *June 1910*

The **BATTLE-LINE** of Languages in Western Europe: A Problem in Human Geography More Perplexing Than That of International Boundaries. By A. L. Guerard. 145-180, *Feb. 1923*

BATTLE MONUMENTS. See War Memorials

BATTLE OF THE BULGE:
Luxembourg, the Quiet Fortress. By Robert Leslie Conly. Photos by Ted H. Funk. 69-97, *July 1970*
Luxembourg, Survivor of Invasions. By Sydney Clark. Photos by Maynard Owen Williams. 791-810, *June 1948*
Belgium Comes Back. By Harvey Klemmer. Photos by Maynard Owen Williams. 575-614, *May 1948*

The **BATTLE** of the Forest. By B. E. Fernow. 127-148, *June 22, 1894*

BATTLEFIELDS:
Gettysburg and Vicksburg: the Battle Towns Today. By Robert Paul Jordan. Map notes by Carolyn Bennett Patterson. Included: Annotated maps charting course of battles. 4-57, *July 1963*
⊕ *Battlefields of the Civil War.* Atlas series. *Apr. 1961*
Our National War Memorials in Europe. By John J. Pershing. 1-36, *Jan. 1934*

The Most Famous Battle Field in America (Gettysburg). Photos by Clifton Adams and Orren R. Louden. 66-75, *July 1931*
Armistice Day and the American Battle Fields. By J. J. Jusserand. Included: The Battle Fields of France Eleven Years After. Photos by Gervais Courtellemont. 509-554, *Nov. 1929*
See also names of battles and wars, *as:* American Revolution; Hastings, Battle of

BATTLE-GROUND of Nature: The Atlantic Seaboard. By John Oliver La Gorce. 511-546, *June 1918*

BATTLESHIPS:
Henry VIII's Lost Warship: *Mary Rose.* By Margaret Rule. Introduction and picture text by Peter Miller. Paintings by Richard Schlecht. 646-675, *May 1983*
Midshipmen's Cruise. By William J. Aston and Alexander G. B. Grosvenor. Included: *New Jersey; Wisconsin.* 711-754, *June 1948*
Your Navy as Peace Insurance. By Chester W. Nimitz. 681-736, *June 1946*
Victory's Portrait in the Marianas. By William Franklin Draper. Paintings by author. 599-616, *Nov. 1945*
Battleship *Missouri* Comes of Age. Photos from U. S. Navy. 353-360, *Mar. 1945*

BATTLING the Juggernaut: Avalanche! By David Cupp. 290-305, *Sept. 1982*

BATTLING with the Panama Slides. By William Joseph Showalter. 133-153, *Feb. 1914*

BAUER, L. A.: *Author*
Most Curious Craft Afloat: The Compass in Navigation and the Work of the Non-Magnetic Yacht "Carnegie." 223-245, *Mar. 1910*
The Magnetic Survey of Africa. 291-297, *Mar. 1909*
The Work in the Pacific Ocean of the Magnetic Survey Yacht "Galilee." 601-611, *Sept. 1907*
The San Francisco Earthquake of April 18, 1906, as Recorded by the Coast and Geodetic Survey Magnetic Observatories. By L. A. Bauer and J. E. Burbank. 298-300, *May 1906*
Magnetic Survey of the Pacific Ocean. 237, *Apr. 1906*
Magnetic Survey of the United States. 92-95, *Mar. 1906*
Magnetic Work of the Coast and Geodetic Survey. 288-289, *Aug. 1899*

BAUER, SIEGBERT: *Photographer*
Behind the Scenes in the Home of the Passion Play (Oberammergau, Germany). 753-760, *Dec. 1935*

BAUM, Ohio:
The Indian Village of Baum. By H. C. Brown. 272-274, *July 1901*

BAUMANN, J. BRUCE: *Photographer*
A Most Uncommon Town: Columbus, Indiana. By David Jeffery. 383-397, *Sept. 1978*

An Eye for an Eye: Pakistan's Wild Frontier. By Mike W. Edwards. 111-139, *Jan. 1977*
Indiana's Self-reliant Uplanders. By James Alexander Thom. 341-363, *Mar. 1976*
The Other Nevada. By Robert Laxalt. 733-761, *June 1974*
Heart of the Bluegrass. By Charles McCarry. 634-659, *May 1974*

BAUXITE:
Aluminum, the Magic Metal. By Thomas Y. Canby. Photos by James L. Amos. 186-211, *Aug. 1978*

BAVARIA (State), West Germany:
Bavaria: Mod, Medieval–and Bewitching. By Gary Jennings. Photos by George F. Mobley. 409-431, *Mar. 1974*
From Chalet to Palace in Bavaria. Photos by Hans Hildenbrand. 683-690, *Dec. 1928*
The Beauty of the Bavarian Alps. By Fitzhugh Lee Minnigerode. 632-649, *June 1926*
The Races of Europe. By Edwin A. Grosvenor. 441-534, *Dec. 1918*
See also Berchtesgaden; Dinkelsbühl; Nördlingen; Oberammergau; Rothenburg

BAVENDAM, FRED: *Photographer*
Mysteries of the Bog. By Louise E. Levathes. Included: Peat holds clues to early American life. 397-420, *Mar. 1987*
Man and Manatee: Can We Live Together? By Alice J. Hall. Included: Man Can Save the Manatee. By Jesse R. White. 400-418, *Sept. 1984*

"BAY OF FIRE." See Phosphorescent Bay

BAYEUX TAPESTRY:
900 Years Ago: the Norman Conquest. By Kenneth M. Setton. Photos by George F. Mobley. The complete Bayeux Tapestry photographed by Milton A. Ford and Victor R. Boswell, Jr. 206-251, *Aug. 1966*
The Beauties of France. By Arthur Stanley Riggs. 391-491, *Nov. 1915*

BAYKAL, Lake, U.S.S.R.:
Siberia: Russia's Frozen Frontier. By Dean Conger. 297-345, *Mar. 1967*
Western Siberia and the Altai Mountains: With Some Speculations on the Future of Siberia. By James Bryce. 469-507, *May 1921*

BAYNES, ERNEST HAROLD: *Author*
Mankind's Best Friend (Dog): Companion of His Solitude, Advance Guard in the Hunt, and Ally of the Trenches. 185-201, *Mar. 1919*
Our Common Dogs. By Louis Agassiz Fuertes and Ernest Harold Baynes. Paintings by Louis Agassiz Fuertes. 201-253, index 280, *Mar. 1919*

BAZAARS:
Peiping's Happy New Year: Lunar Celebration Attracts Throngs to Temple Fairs, Motley Bazaars, and Age-old Festivities. By George Kin Leung. 749-792, *Dec. 1936*

CARMICHAEL, LEONARD:
NGS Committee for Research and Exploration: Chairman. 882, Dec. 1961; 903, Dec. 1962; 9, 136, 146, 150, Jan. 1963; 626, Oct. 1963; 582, Oct. 1967; 230, Aug. 1970; 274, Aug. 1982
Leonard Carmichael: An Appreciation. By Melvin M. Payne. 871-874, Dec. 1973
Nomination Page. July 1970
Nomination Page. July 1969
Nomination Page. Sept. 1965
NGS Vice President for Research and Exploration. 525, Apr. 1965
Nomination Page. May 1964
NGS Board of Trustees. 419, 420, 423, Mar. 1957; 592, May 1957; 834, Dec. 1959; 796-797, June 1960; 881, 883, Dec. 1960
Nomination Page. May 1960
Author
The Smithsonian, Magnet on the Mall. Photos by Volkmar Wentzel. 796-845, June 1960

CARMICHAEL, PETER:
Photographer
Scotland, Ghosts, and Glory. By Rowe Findley. 40-69, July 1984

CARNEGIE, ANDREW:
The Discovery of the North Pole. Speech by Andrew Carnegie. 63-82, Jan. 1910

CARNEGIE, DAVID J.: Photographer
Weighing the Aga Khan in Diamonds. 317-324, Mar. 1947

CARNEGIE (Yacht):
Sailing the Seven Seas in the Interest of Science: Adventures Through 157,000 Miles of Storm and Calm, from Arctic to Antarctic and Around the World, in the Non-magnetic Yacht "Carnegie." By J. P. Ault. 631-690, Dec. 1922
Most Curious Craft Afloat: The Compass in Navigation and the Work of the Non-Magnetic Yacht "Carnegie." By L. A. Bauer. 223-245, Mar. 1910

CARNEGIE INSTITUTION OF WASHINGTON:
The Carnegie Institution. 124, Feb. 1908
Geologists in China. 640-644, Oct. 1907
Recent Magnetic Work by the Carnegie Institution of Washington. 648, Nov. 1906
See also Carnegie (Yacht)

CARNIVAL (Pre-Lenten Festival):
Brazil: Moment of Promise and Pain. By Priit J. Vesilind. Photos by Stephanie Maze. Included: Carnival in Rio de Janeiro. 348-385, Mar. 1987
Marking Time in Grenada. By Charles E. Cobb, Jr. Photos by David Alan Harvey. 688-710, Nov. 1984
Carnival in Trinidad. By Howard La Fay. Photos by Winfield Parks. 693-701, Nov. 1971
Brazil, Ôba! By Peter T. White. Photos by Winfield Parks. 299-353, Sept. 1962
Spectacular Rio de Janeiro. By Hernane

Tavares de Sá. Photos by Charles Allmon. 289-328, Mar. 1955
Rio Panorama: Breath-taking Is This Fantastic City amid Peaks, Palms, and Sea, and in Carnival Time It Moves to the Rhythm of Music. By W. Robert Moore. Included: Carioca Carnival. 283-324, Sept. 1939
Carnival Days on the Riviera. By Maynard Owen Williams. 467-501, Oct. 1926
See also Mardi Gras

CARNIVALS. See Fairs; Festivals

CARNIVORES of a Lightless World (Fishes). Paintings by Else Bostelmann and E. J. Geske. 693-700, Dec. 1934

CARNIVOROUS PLANTS:
Malaysia's Giant Flowers and Insect-trapping Plants. By Paul A. Zahl. 680-701, May 1964
Plants That Eat Insects. By Paul A. Zahl. 643-659, May 1961

CAROLINE ISLANDS, Pacific Ocean:
In the Far Pacific: At the Birth of Nations. By Carolyn Bennett Patterson. Photos by David Hiser and Melinda Berge. Note: The Caroline Islands, stretching 2,000 miles from Palau to Kosrae, are divided politically into the Republic of Palau and the Federated States of Micronesia. 460-499, Oct. 1986
Micronesia: The Americanization of Eden. By David S. Boyer. 702-744, May 1967
Pacific Wards of Uncle Sam. By W. Robert Moore. 73-104, July 1948
American Pathfinders in the Pacific. By William H. Nicholas. 617-640, May 1946
South from Saipan. By W. Robert Moore. 441-474, Apr. 1945
Hidden Key to the Pacific: Piercing the Web of Secrecy Which Long Has Veiled Japanese Bases in the Mandated Islands. By Willard Price. 759-785, June 1942
Yap and Other Pacific Islands under Japanese Mandate. By Junius B. Wood. 591-627, Dec. 1921
The Caroline Islands. 227, June 1899
See also Ifalik; Kapingamarangi; Palau; Truk Islands; Ulithi; Yap

CARONI SWAMP SANCTUARY, Trinidad:
New Scarlet Bird in Florida Skies. By Paul A. Zahl. 874-882, Dec. 1967

CARPATHIAN MOUNTAINS, Europe:
Americans Afoot in Rumania. By Dan Dimancescu. Photos by Dick Durrance II and Christopher G. Knight. 810-845, June 1969
See also Tatra Mountains

CARPENTER, FRANK G.:
Awarded Jane M. Smith Life Membership. 342, Apr. 1920

CARPENTER, RHYS: Author
Ancient Rome Brought to Life. Paintings by H. M. Herget. 567-633, Nov. 1946

CARR, ARCHIE: Author
Imperiled Gift of the Sea: Caribbean Green Turtle. Photos by Robert E. Schroeder. 876-890, June 1967
Alligators: Dragons in Distress. Photos by Treat Davidson and Laymond Hardy. 133-148, Jan. 1967

CARR, GERALD P.:
Skylab, Outpost on the Frontier of Space. By Thomas Y. Canby. Photos by the nine mission astronauts. 441-469, Oct. 1974

CARRAO, Río, Venezuela:
Jungle Journey to the World's Highest Waterfall. By Ruth Robertson. 655-690, Nov. 1949

CARRARA MARBLE:
Carrara Marble: Touchstone of Eternity. By Cathy Newman. Photos by Pierre Boulat. 42-59, July 1982

CARRIERS, Airplane. See Aircraft Carriers; Escort Carriers

CARRYING the Color Camera Through Unmapped China. Photos by Joseph F. Rock. 403-434, Oct. 1930

CARRYING Water Through a Desert: The Story of the Los Angeles Aqueduct. By Burt A. Heinly. 568-596, July 1910

CARROLL, ALLEN:
Graphics Designer
The Smell Survey Results. By Avery N. Gilbert and Charles J. Wysocki. Graphics designed by Allen Carroll and painted by Mark Seidler. 514-525, Oct. 1987
The World's Urban Explosion. By Robert W. Fox. 179-185, Aug. 1984

CARS. See Automobiles

CARSON, Camp, Colorado:
School for Survival. By Curtis E. LeMay. 565-602, May 1953

CARSON CITY, Nevada:
Nevada, Desert Treasure House. By W. Robert Moore. 1-38, Jan. 1946

CARTAGO, Costa Rica:
Costa Rica–Vulcan's Smithy. By H. Pittier. 494-525, June 1910

CARTER, JEFF: Photographer
"The Alice" in Australia's Wonderland. By Alan Villiers. Photos by Jeff Carter and David Moore. 230-257, Feb. 1966

CARTER, T. DONALD: Author
Stalking Central Africa's Wildlife. Paintings by Walter A. Weber. 264-286, Aug. 1956

CARTER, WILLIAM HARDING:
Author
The Story of the Horse: The Development of Man's Companion in War Camp, on Farm, in the Marts of Trade, and in the Field of Sports. Paintings by Edward Herbert Miner. 455-566, Nov. 1923
■ The Horses of the World: The Development of Man's Companion in War

Sample Page

East Germany: The Struggle to Succeed. By John J. Putman. Photos by Gordon W. Gahan. 295-329, *Sept. 1974*
Berlin, on Both Sides of the Wall. By Howard Sochurek. 1-47, *Jan. 1970*
See also Ströbeck

GERMANY, West:
A Wild, Ill-fated Balloon Race. 778-797. Included: Last Ascent of a Heroic Team (Maxie Anderson and Don Ida). 794-797, *Dec. 1983*
Two Berlins–A Generation Apart. By Priit J. Vesilind. Photos by Cotton Coulson. Note: Although not a constituent part of West Germany but a protectorate of France, Great Britain, and the United States, West Berlin is dependent on funds from Bonn. 2-51, *Jan. 1982*
The Danube: River of Many Nations, Many Names. By Mike Edwards. Photos by Winfield Parks. 455-485, *Oct. 1977*
West Germany: Continuing Miracle. By John J. Putman. Photos by Robert W. Madden. 149-181, *Aug. 1977*
Bavaria: Mod, Medieval–and Bewitching. By Gary Jennings. Photos by George F. Mobley. 409-431, *Mar. 1974*
The Rhine: Europe's River of Legend. By William Graves. Photos by Bruce Dale. 449-499, *Apr. 1967*
The Alps: Man's Own Mountains. By Ralph Gray. Photos by Walter Meayers Edwards and William Eppridge. 350-395, *Sept. 1965*
Down the Danube by Canoe. By William Slade Backer. Photos by Richard S. Durrance and Christopher G. Knight. 34-79, *July 1965*
Life in Walled-off West Berlin. By Nathaniel T. Kenney and Volkmar Wentzel. Photos by Thomas Nebbia. 735-767, *Dec. 1961*
Modern Miracle, Made in Germany. By Robert Leslie Conly. Photos by Erich Lessing. 735-791, *June 1959*
See also Berchtesgaden; Dinkelsbühl; Freiburg; Hamburg; Helgoland (Island); Nördlingen; Oberammergau; Rothenburg

GERRHA (Ancient City), Saudi Arabia:
In Search of Arabia's Past. By Peter Bruce Cornwall. 493-522, *Apr. 1948*

GERSTER, GEORG:
Nomination Page. In Egypt. *May 1966*
Author-Photographer
Tsetse–Fly of the Deadly Sleep. 814-833, *Dec. 1986*
Patterns of Plenty: The Art in Farming. 391-399, *Sept. 1984*
The Niger: River of Sorrow, River of Hope. 152-189, *Aug. 1975*
Searching Out Medieval Churches in Ethiopia's Wilds. 856-884, *Dec. 1970*
Abu Simbel's Ancient Temples Reborn. 724-744, *May 1969*
Saving the Ancient Temples at Abu Simbel. Paintings by Robert W. Nicholson. 694-742, *May 1966*

Threatened Treasures of the Nile. 587-621, *Oct. 1963*
Photographer
Egypt's Desert of Promise. By Farouk El-Baz. 190-221, *Feb. 1982*
The Desert: An Age-old Challenge Grows. By Rick Gore. Photos by Georg Gerster and Bruce Dale. 586-639, *Nov. 1979*
Salt–The Essence of Life. By Gordon Young. Photos by Volkmar Wentzel and Georg Gerster. 381-401, *Sept. 1977*

GESKE, E. J.: *Artist*
Marvels of Fern Life. 547-562, *May 1925*
Author-Artist
Familiar Grasses and Their Flowers. By E. J. Geske and W. J. Showalter. Included: Beauties of Our Common Grasses. 625-636, *June 1921*

GETTING to Know the Wild Burros of Death Valley. By Patricia des Roses Moehlman. Photos by Ira S. Lerner and author. 502-517, *Apr. 1972*

GETTYSBURG, Pennsylvania:
Gettysburg and Vicksburg: the Battle Towns Today. By Robert Paul Jordan. Map notes by Carolyn Bennett Patterson. 4-57, *July 1963*
The Most Famous Battle Field in America. Photos by Clifton Adams and Orren R. Louden. 66-75, *July 1931*

GEYRE, Turkey:
Ancient Aphrodisias Lives Through Its Art. By Kenan T. Erim. Photos by David Brill. NGS research grant. 527-551, *Oct. 1981*

GEYSERS:
Fabulous Yellowstone: Even Stranger Than the Tales of Early Trappers is the Truth About This Steaming Wonderland. By Frederick G. Vosburgh. 769-794, *June 1940*
Waimangu and the Hot-Spring Country of New Zealand: The World's Greatest Geyser Is One of Many Natural Wonders in a Land of Inferno and Vernal Paradise. By Joseph C. Grew. 109-130, *Aug. 1925*
Costa Rica–Vulcan's Smithy. By H. Pittier. 494-525, *June 1910*
See also Iceland; Yellowstone

GHANA:
Africa: The Winds of Freedom Stir a Continent. By Nathaniel T. Kenney. Photos by W. D. Vaughn. 303-359, *Sept. 1960*
See also former name, Gold Coast

GHARIALS:
A Bad Time to Be a Crocodile. By Rick Gore. Photos by Jonathan Blair. 90-115, *Jan. 1978*

GHAZNI, Afghanistan:
Back to Afghanistan. By Maynard Owen Williams. 517-544, *Oct. 1946*

GHOST From the Depths: the Warship *Vasa*. By Anders Franzén. 42-57, *Jan. 1962*

GHOST Ships of the War of 1812: *Hamilton* and *Scourge*. By Daniel A. Nelson. Photos by Emory Kristof. Paintings by Richard Schlecht. Included: The Incredible Crawl of Ned Myers. 289-313, *Mar. 1983*

The **GHOSTS** of Jericho. By James L. Kelso. 825-844, *Dec. 1951*

GHOSTS of the Gulf Stream: Blue-water Plankton. By William M. Hamner. 530-545, *Oct. 1974*

GHOSTS of War in the South Pacific. By Peter Benchley. Photos by David Doubilet. 424-457, *Apr. 1988*

GHOSTS on the Little Bighorn. By Robert Paul Jordan. Photos by Scott Rutherford. 787-813, *Dec. 1986*

GIANT AFRICAN LAND SNAILS:
Formosa–Hot Spot of the East. By Frederick G. Vosburgh. Photos by J. Baylor Roberts. 139-176, *Feb. 1950*

GIANT Brazil. By Peter T. White. Photos by Winfield Parks. 299-353, *Sept. 1962*

GIANT BRAZILIAN OTTERS:
Giant Otters: "Big Water Dogs" in Peril. By Nicole Duplaix. Photos by the author and Bates Littlehales. NGS research grant. 130-142, *July 1980*

GIANT Comet Grazes the Sun. By Kenneth F. Weaver. 259-261, *Feb. 1966*

GIANT EARTHWORMS:
Capturing Strange Creatures in Colombia. By Marte Latham. Photos by Tor Eigeland. 682-693, *May 1966*

GIANT Effigies of the Southwest. By George C. Marshall. 389, *Sept. 1952*

GIANT FOREST, Sequoia National Park, California:
Giant Sequoias Draw Millions to California Parks. By John Michael Kauffmann. Photos by B. Anthony Stewart. 147-187, *Aug. 1959*
Saving Earth's Oldest Living Things. By Andrew H. Brown. Photos by Raymond Moulin and author. 679-695, *May 1951*

GIANT FROGS:
In Quest of the World's Largest Frog. By Paul A. Zahl. 146-152, *July 1967*

GIANT Insects of the Amazon. By Paul A. Zahl. 632-669, *May 1959*

GIANT KELP:
Undersea World of a Kelp Forest. By Sylvia A. Earle. Photos by Al Giddings. 411-426, *Sept. 1980*
Giant Kelp, Sequoias of the Sea. By Wheeler J. North. Photos by Bates Littlehales. 251-269, *Aug. 1972*

GIANT PANDAS:
Secrets of the Wild Panda. By George B. Schaller. 284-309, *Mar. 1986*
● Save the Panda. 824, *Dec. 1982*; cover, *Mar. 1983*
Pandas in the Wild. By George B. Schaller. 735-749, *Dec. 1981*
What's Black and White and Loved All

Sample Page

RIYADH

Life's Pattern on the Italian Riviera. By Helen Churchill Candee. 67-100, *Jan. 1935*

Carnival Days on the Riviera. By Maynard Owen Williams. 467-501, *Oct. 1926*

RIYADH, Saudi Arabia:

Saudi Arabia: The Kingdom and Its Power. By Robert Azzi. 286-333, *Sept. 1980*

Guest in Saudi Arabia. By Maynard Owen Williams. 463-487, *Oct. 1945*

ROACHES. *See* Cockroaches

The **ROAD** of the Crusaders: A Historian Follows the Steps of Richard the Lion Heart and Other Knights of the Cross Over the "Via Dei." By Harold Lamb. 645-693, *Dec. 1933*

The **ROAD** to Bolivia. By William E. Curtis. 209-224, June 1900; 264-280, *July 1900*

The **ROAD** to Wang Ye Fu: An Account of the Work of the National Geographic Society's Central-China Expedition in the Mongol Kingdom of Ala Shan. By Frederick R. Wulsin. 197-234, *Feb. 1926*

ROADRUNNERS:

The Roadrunner–Clown of the Desert. By Martha A. Whitson. Photos by Bruce Dale. 694-702, *May 1983*

ROADS. *See* Highways and Roads

ROADS from Washington. By John Patric. 1-56, *July 1938*

ROAMING Africa's Unfenced Zoos. By W. Robert Moore. 353-380, *Mar. 1950*

ROAMING India's Naga Hills. By S. Dillon Ripley. 247-264, *Feb. 1955*

ROAMING Korea South of the Iron Curtain. By Enzo de Chetelat. 777-808, *June 1950*

ROAMING Russia's Caucasus: Rugged Mountains and Hardy Fighters Guard the Soviet Union's Caucasian Treasury of Manganese and Oil. By Rolf Singer. 91-121, *July 1942*

ROAMING the West's Fantastic Four Corners. By Jack Breed. 705-742, *June 1952*

ROAN MOUNTAIN, North Carolina-Tennessee:

Rhododendron Time on Roan Mountain. By Ralph Gray. 819-828, *June 1957*

ROANOKE ISLAND, North Carolina:

Lonely Cape Hatteras, Besieged by the Sea. By William S. Ellis. Photos by Emory Kristof. 393-421, *Sept. 1969*

October Holiday on the Outer Banks. By Nike Anderson. Photos by J. Baylor Roberts. 501-529, *Oct. 1955*

Exploring America's Great Sand Barrier Reef. By Eugene R. Guild. Photos by John E. Fletcher and author. 325-350, *Sept. 1947*

Indian Life Before the Colonists Came. By Stuart E. Jones. Engravings by

Theodore de Bry (1590). 351-368, *Sept. 1947*

A Bit of Elizabethan England in America: Fisher Folk of the Islands Off North Carolina Conserved the Speech and Customs of Sir Walter Raleigh's Colonists. By Blanch Nettleton Epler. 695-730, *Dec. 1933*

ROBBINS, MICHAEL: *Author*

■■ *High Country Trail: Along the Continental Divide.* Photos by Paul Chesley. 199 pages. *1981*

ROBERT COLLEGE, Turkey:

Robert College, Turkish Gateway to the Future. By Franc Shor. 399-418, *Sept. 1957*

American Alma Maters in the Near East. By Maynard Owen Williams. 237-256, *Aug. 1945*

ROBERT FROST and New England. By Archibald MacLeish. 438-444, *Apr. 1976*

ROBERT REDFORD Rides the Outlaw Trail. By Robert Redford. Photos by Jonathan Blair. 622-657, *Nov. 1976*

ROBERT V. FLEMING, 1890-1967. By Melville Bell Grosvenor. 526-529, *Apr. 1968*

ROBERTS, FRANK H. H., Jr.: *Author*

In the Empire of the Aztecs: Mexico City Is Rich in Relics of a People Who Practiced Human Sacrifice, Yet Loved Flowers, Education, and Art. Paintings by H. M. Herget. 725-750, *June 1937*

ROBERTS, J. BAYLOR:

Nomination Page. *Nov. 1960*

Author-Photographer

Focusing on the Tournament of Roses. By B. Anthony Stewart and J. Baylor Roberts. 805-816, *June 1954*

Photographer

Scientists Drill at Sea to Pierce Earth's Crust. By Samuel W. Matthews. Contents: Project Mohole. 686-697, *Nov. 1961*

Triton Follows Magellan's Wake. By Edward L. Beach. 585-615, *Nov. 1960*

Bounty Descendants Live on Remote Norfolk Island. By T. C. Roughley. 559-584, *Oct. 1960*

The Night the Mountains Moved. By Samuel W. Matthews. 329-359, *Mar. 1960*

Iraq–Where Oil and Water Mix. By Jean and Franc Shor. 443-489, *Oct. 1958*

Heritage of Beauty and History. By Conrad L. Wirth. 587-661, *May 1958*

Slow Boat to Florida. By Dorothea and Stuart E. Jones. 1-65, *Jan. 1958*

Charting Our Sea and Air Lanes. By Stuart E. Jones. 189-209, *Feb. 1957*

Our Green Treasury, the National Forests. By Nathaniel T. Kenney. 287-324, *Sept. 1956*

Hunting the Heartbeat of a Whale. By Paul Dudley White and Samuel W. Matthews. 49-64, *July 1956*

October Holiday on the Outer Banks. By Nike Anderson. 501-529, *Oct. 1955*

This Young Giant, Indonesia. By Beverley M. Bowie. 351-392, *Sept. 1955*

Across Canada by Mackenzie's Track. By Ralph Gray. 191-239, *Aug. 1955*

Saving Man's Wildlife Heritage. By John H. Baker. 581-620, *Nov. 1954*

America Goes to the Fair. By Samuel W. Matthews. 293-333, *Sept. 1954*

New Rush to Golden California. By George W. Long. 723-802, *June 1954*

Hong Kong Hangs On. By George W. Long. 239-272, *Feb. 1954*

Cruising Japan's Inland Sea. By Willard Price. 619-650, *Nov. 1953*

Our Navy in the Far East. By Arthur W. Radford. 537-577, *Oct. 1953*

Macau, a Hole in the Bamboo Curtain. By George W. Long. 679-688, *May 1953*

Malaya Meets Its Emergency. By George W. Long. 185-228, *Feb. 1953*

La Jolla, a Gem of the California Coast. By Deena Clark. 755-782, *Dec. 1952*

Indochina Faces the Dragon. By George W. Long. 287-328, *Sept. 1952*

"Around the World in Eighty Days." By Newman Bumstead. 705-750, *Dec. 1951*

Journey Into Troubled Iran. By George W. Long. 425-464, *Oct. 1951*

North Dakota Comes into Its Own. By Leo A. Borah. 283-322, *Sept. 1951*

Dog Mart Day in Fredericksburg. By Frederick G. Vosburgh. 817-832, *June 1951*

Seeing the Earth from 80 Miles Up. By Clyde T. Holliday. 511-528, *Oct. 1950*

Japan Tries Freedom's Road. By Frederick G. Vosburgh. 593-632, *May 1950*

Formosa–Hot Spot of the East. By Frederick G. Vosburgh. 139-176, *Feb. 1950*

From Indian Canoes to Submarines at Key West. By Frederick Simpich. 41-72, *Jan. 1950*

Pittsburgh: Workshop of the Titans. By Albert W. Atwood. 117-144, *July 1949*

Dixie Spins the Wheel of Industry. By William H. Nicholas. 281-324, *Mar. 1949*

Uncle Sam Bends a Twig in Germany. By Frederick Simpich. 529-550, *Oct. 1948*

Around the "Great Lakes of the South." By Frederick Simpich. 463-491, *Apr. 1948*

The Wonder City That Moves by Night. By Francis Beverly Kelley. 289-324, *Mar. 1948*

Shawneetown Forsakes the Ohio. By William H. Nicholas. 273-288, *Feb. 1948*

Carnival in San Antonio. By Mason Sutherland. 813-844, *Dec. 1947*

Louisiana Trades with the World. By Frederick Simpich. 705-738, *Dec. 1947*

Men, Moose, and Mink of Northwest Angle. By William H. Nicholas. 265-284, *Aug. 1947*

Deep in the Heart of "Swissconsin." By William H. Nicholas. 781-800, *June 1947*

© 1990 by The Center for Applied Research in Education

TURKISTAN

Valley, Plateau Paradise of Mongol and Turkic Tribes. By Edward Murray. Paintings and drawings by Alexandre Iacovleff. 1-57, *Jan. 1936*
See also Tatars; Turkomans

TURKISTAN. *See* Sinkiang; Soviet Central Asia

TURKMEN SOVIET SOCIALIST REPUBLIC:
The Afghan Borderland. By Ellsworth Huntington. Part I: The Russian Frontier. 788-799, *Sept. 1909*
Life in the Great Desert of Central Asia. By Ellsworth Huntington. 749-760, *Aug. 1909*

TURKOMANS:
Bold Horsemen of the Steppes. By Sabrina and Roland Michaud. 634-669, *Nov. 1973*
Russia's Orphan Races: Picturesque Peoples Who Cluster on the Southeastern Borderland of the Vast Slav Dominions. By Maynard Owen Williams. 245-278, *Oct. 1918*
Life in the Great Desert of Central Asia. By Ellsworth Huntington. 749-760, *Aug. 1909*

TURKS:
Cyprus Under Four Flags: A Struggle for Unity. By Kenneth MacLeish. Photos by Jonathan Blair. 356-383, *Mar. 1973*
The Isles of Greece: Aegean Birthplace of Western Culture. By Melville Bell Grosvenor. Photos by Edwin Stuart Grosvenor and Winfield Parks. 147-193, *Aug. 1972*

TURKU ARCHIPELAGO, Finland:
Scenes of Postwar Finland. By La Verne Bradley. Photos by Jerry Waller. 233-264, *Aug. 1947*

TURNAROUND Time in West Virginia. By Elizabeth A. Moize. Photos by Jodi Cobb. 755-785, *June 1976*

TURNER, DANIEL S.: *Photographer*
Voyage of the *Morrissey*. Photos by Daniel S. Turner and Sherman A. Wengerd. 609-616, *May 1946*

TURNER, J. HENRY: *Author*
The Alaskan Boundary Survey. III–The Boundary North of Fort Yukon. 189-197, *Feb. 8, 1893*

TURNING Back Time in the South Seas. By Thor Heyerdahl. Contents: Fatu-Hiva Island. 109-136, *Jan. 1941*

TURNLEY, DAVID:
On Assignment in South Africa. *Oct. 1988*
Photographer
The Afrikaners. By André Brink. 556-585, *Oct. 1988*

TUROCZ SZENT MARTIN, Czechoslovakia. *See* Turciansky Svaty Martin

TURPAN DEPRESSION (Region), China:
Journey to China's Far West. By Rick

Gore. Photos by Bruce Dale. 292-331, *Mar. 1980*

TURTLE BOGUE. *See* Tortuguero Beach, Costa Rica

TURTLES:
Freshwater Turtles–Designed for Survival. By Christopher P. White. Photos by Bill Curtsinger. Contents: Alligator snapper, Black-knobbed sawback, Common snapping, Eastern painted, Gulf Coast spiny softshell, Map turtle, Painted, Peninsula cooter, Plymouth red-belly white, River cooter, Softshell, Spotted, Stinkpot, Stripe-necked musk, Suwannee cooter, Yellow-belly sliders, Yellow-blotched sawback. 40-59, *Jan. 1986*
One Strange Night on Turtle Beach. By Paul A. Zahl. 570-581, *Oct. 1973*
In the Wilds of a City Parlor. By Paul A. Zahl. 645-672, *Nov. 1954*
Nature's Tank, the Turtle. By Doris M. Cochran. Paintings by Walter A. Weber. 665-684, *May 1952*
Capturing Giant Turtles in the Caribbean. By David D. Duncan. 177-190, *Aug. 1943*
Certain Citizens of the Warm Sea. By Louis L. Mowbray. Paintings by Hashime Murayama. 27-62, *Jan. 1922*
Reptiles of All Lands. By Raymond L. Ditmars. 601-633, *July 1911*
Notes on the Remarkable Habits of Certain Turtles and Lizards. By H. A. Largelamb (Alexander Graham Bell). 413-419, *June 1907*
Cultivation of Marine and Fresh-Water Animals in Japan. By K. Mitsukuri. 524-531, *Sept. 1906*
See also Green Turtles; Tortoises

TUSCANY (Region), Italy:
The Eternal Etruscans. By Rick Gore. Photos by O. Louis Mazzatenta. Paintings by James M. Gurney. 696-743, *June 1988*
Carrara Marble: Touchstone of Eternity. By Cathy Newman. Photos by Pierre Boulat. 42-59, *July 1982*
Leonardo da Vinci: A Man for All Ages. By Kenneth MacLeish. Photos by James L. Amos. 296-329, *Sept. 1977*
The Renaissance Lives On in Tuscany. By Luis Marden. Photos by Albert Moldvay. 626-659, *Nov. 1974*
Italy, From Roman Ruins to Radio: History of Ancient Bridge Building and Road Making Repeats Itself in Modern Public Works and Engineering Projects. By John Patric. 347-394, *Mar. 1940*
Holidays Among the Hill Towns of Umbria and Tuscany. By Paul Wilstach. 401-442, *Apr. 1928*
Inexhaustible Italy. By Arthur Stanley Riggs. 273-368, *Oct. 1916*
See also Florence; Siena

TUSCARORA DEEP, Pacific Ocean:
The Recent Earthquake Wave on the Coast of Japan. By Eliza Ruhamah Scidmore. 285-289, *Sept. 1896*
Reports of Sealing Schooners Cruising in the Neighborhood of Tuscarora Deep in May and June, 1896. By

Eliza Ruhamah Scidmore. 310-312, *Sept. 1896*

TUSCARORA INDIANS:
"The Fire That Never Dies." By Harvey Arden. Photos by Steve Wall. 375-403, *Sept. 1987*

TUSHINGHAM, A. DOUGLAS:
Author
The Men Who Hid the Dead Sea Scrolls. Paintings by Peter V. Bianchi. 785-808, *Dec. 1958*
Jericho Gives Up Its Secrets. By Kathleen M. Kenyon and A. Douglas Tushingham. Photos by Nancy Lord. 853-870, *Dec. 1953*

TUTANKHAMUN:
■ *Ancient Egypt: Discovering its Splendors.* 256 pages. *1978*
Dazzling Legacy of an Ancient Quest. By Alice J. Hall. 293-311, *Mar. 1977*
Golden Masterpieces. 36-39, *Jan. 1974*
Tutankhamun's Golden Trove. By Christiane Desroches Noblecourt. Photos by F. L. Kenett. 625-646, *Oct. 1963*
At the Tomb of Tutankhamen: An Account of the Opening of the Royal Egyptian Sepulcher. By Maynard Owen Williams. 461-508, *May 1923*

TUTTLE, MERLIN D.:
President's Page. By Gilbert M. Grosvenor. *Feb. 1987*
On Assignment in Kenya. *Apr. 1986*
On Assignment in Thailand. *Jan. 1982*
Author-Photographer
Gentle Fliers of the African Night. Contents: Bats. NGS research grant. 540-558, *Apr. 1986*
The Amazing Frog-Eating Bat. 78-91, *Jan. 1982*

TUTUILA (Island), American Samoa, Pacific Ocean:
The Two Samoas, Still Coming of Age. By Robert Booth. Photos by Melinda Berge. 452-473, *Oct. 1985*
America's South Sea Soldiers. By Lorena MacIntyre Quinn. 267-274, *Sept. 1919*

TUVALU. *See* former name, Ellice Islands

TWAIN, MARK:
Editorial. By Gilbert M. Grosvenor. 577, *May 1976*
Editorial. By Gilbert M. Grosvenor. 299, *Sept. 1975*
Mark Twain: Mirror of America. By Noel Grove. Photos by James L. Stanfield. 300-337, *Sept. 1975*
Tom Sawyer's Town. By Jerry Allen. 121-140, *July 1956*
The West Through Boston Eyes. By Stewart Anderson. Included: Today in Mark Twain's Home Town; Exploring Tom Sawyer's Cave. 733-776, *June 1949*

TWEED:
From Barra to Butt in the Hebrides. By Isobel Wylie Hutchison. 559-580, *Oct. 1954*
Over the Sea to Scotland's Skye. By Robert J. Reynolds. 87-112, *July 1952*

GUIDE WORD PUZZLES

Skill Reinforced

Identifying which words belong between given guide words

Type of Activity

Whole class game, small group game, or center

Grade Level: 3–4

Time Required

One session for puzzle construction; one session minimum for playing

Prerequisite

Introduction to guide words

Materials

Lined paper for word lists
Puzzles A–F, reproduced onto cardstock (each child should have one puzzle)
Pencils and pens or felt markers
Dictionaries (at least one per group)
Letter size envelopes (one per puzzle)
Paper clips
Scissors

Puzzle Construction

1. Divide class into groups of two to four.

2. Assign guide words (see sample list) to each group.

3. Using the dictionaries, students find words that belong on their "page," and one student lists the words on a sheet of lined paper. Enough words should be recorded so each student can use different words. That means a group of two needs sixteen words, three needs twenty-four words, and four needs thirty-two.

4. Students should check their lists and make sure each word passes the following two tests:
   Test 1. Does the word come AFTER the first guide word?
   Test 2. Does the word come BEFORE the last guide word?
   If the answer is yes to both tests, the word can be used. If the answer is no, a new word that passes the two tests should be found and added to the list.

5. Hand out a blank puzzle to each child.

6. Students should write the guide words on the lines in the appropriate corners at the top of the puzzle.

7. Using the word list, students write one word in each puzzle piece.

8. Students should carefully cut out the frame and pieces and lightly label the back of each puzzle piece and the frame with their name.

9. The pieces should be placed in an envelope and the envelope paper clipped to the frame.

10. Puzzles can be laminated, if desired.

Procedure for Playing

1. Select two puzzles for each group. The beginning letter of one of the guide words should be the same, for example, able–bounce and bow–drum. Also, the puzzles should not both have the same pattern.

2. The students mix up the pieces for the two puzzles. They look at each piece to decide which set of guide words it belongs under and place the piece on the correct "page."

3. To check their answers, they put the puzzle together. If the puzzle does not fit together correctly, the students should recheck each word with the guide words.

4. With six puzzle designs and a variety of words and guide words, this activity can be used in many different combinations.

Sample List of Guide Words

able–bounce	fence–great	meat–open	think–tree
bow–drum	green–hole	or–seed	trick–zoo
dry–feet	home–meal	seem–thing	

Follow-up Activities

BEFORE, AFTER, OR ON THAT PAGE! (see CHOOSE AND CHECK)
WHICH VOLUME?

Guide Word Puzzle A

Guide Word Puzzle B

Guide Word Puzzle C

Guide Word Puzzle D

Guide Word Puzzle E

Guide Word Puzzle F

FROM WHICH TREE DID I FALL?

Skills Reinforced

Practice using guide words
Practice recognizing call numbers used in the LMC (variation)
Practice organizing information (variation)

Type of Activity

Whole class game (bulletin board activity)
Small group or individual paper and pencil activity

Grade Level: 2+

Time Required

One session

Prerequisites

Introduction to guide words, or
AROUND THE WORLD
THAT'S A FACT; LET YOUR KNOWLEDGE BLOSSOM!

Materials

Bulletin board
Five trees reproduced onto brown card stock and cut out
Labels for trees reproduced and cut out
Leaves reproduced onto yellow, red, and orange colored card stock, cut out, and laminated
Letters for title of bulletin board (not provided)
Straight pins or stapler

From Which Tree Did I fall?

Procedure

1. Place trees and title, "From Which Tree Did I Fall?", on the bulletin board.
2. Label each tree with a guide word label.
3. Distribute a leaf with a word on it and a straight pin (or use a stapler) to each student.
4. Each student looks at the word on the leaf and the labels on the trees to determine which tree the leaf could have come from.
5. One by one the students show and tell the class where the leaves belong. If correct, the student pins or staples the leaf near the tree as if it were falling from it. If incorrect, discussion from the class helps the student to decide more appropriately.

Variations

- Call Number Recognition: The procedure is the same as above, except use the LMC labels instead of the guide word labels and call number leaves instead of word leaves.
- Another possibility is to reproduce the call number leaf sheets onto white paper and have students color leaves according to a chart, e.g.

fiction	orange
nonfiction	yellow
reference	red
picture book	green
AV	brown

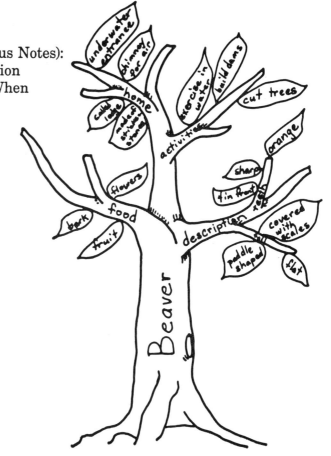

Organizing Information (Treemendous Notes): Provide students with a reproduction of a bare tree and blank leaves. When researching a subject, students write one fact on each leaf. When notes are finished, they cut out each leaf, group like notes together, and determine a heading for each group of notes. The students write the main topic of their research on the tree trunk and the various headings on the limbs. They can then glue the leaves onto the appropriate limbs.

Follow-up Activities

WHICH VOLUME?

From Which
Tree Did
I Fall?

From Which Tree Did I Fall?

Guide Word Labels

about – drop

drug – heat

heave – orbit

order – sock

soft – zoom

LMC Labels

Fiction

Nonfiction

Reference

Picture Book

Audio–Visual

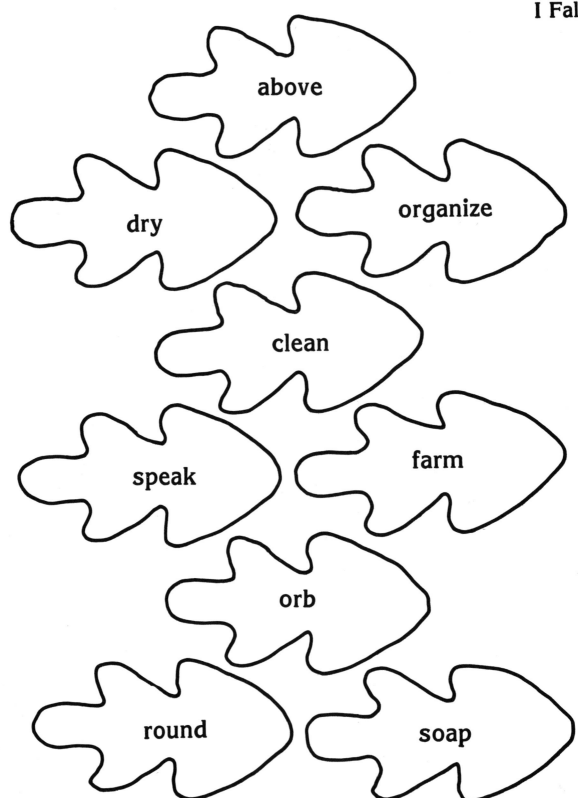

above

dry

organize

clean

speak

farm

orb

round

soap

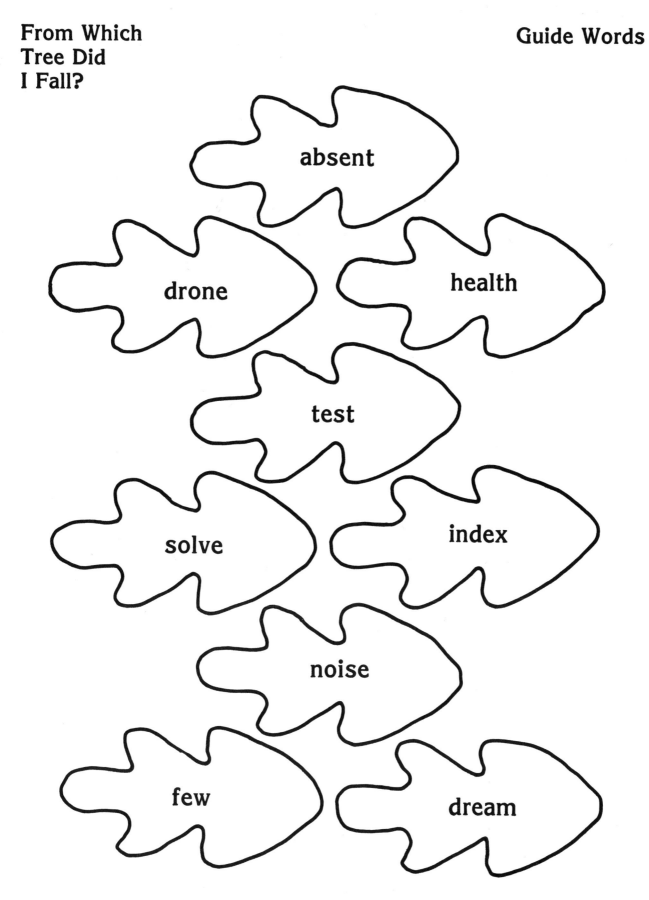

absent

drone

health

test

solve

index

noise

few

dream

Guide Words

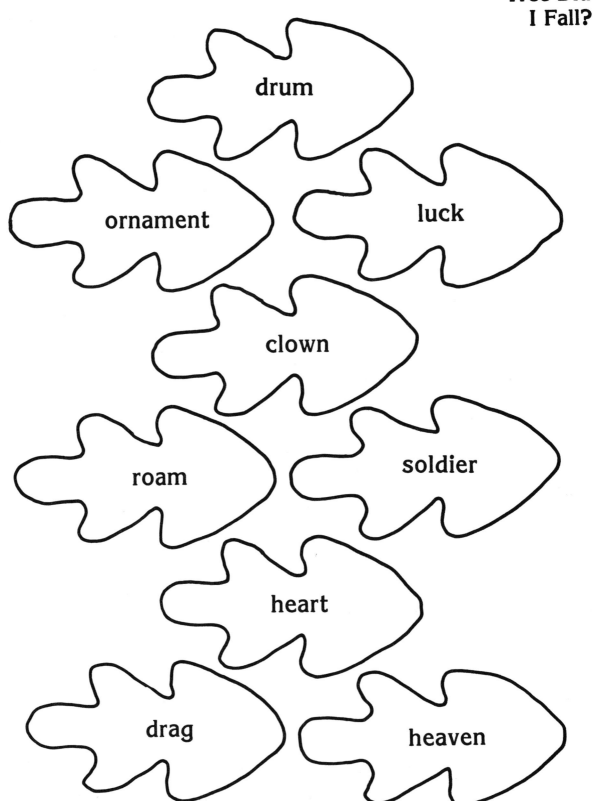

drum

ornament

luck

clown

roam

soldier

heart

drag

heaven

From Which Tree Did I Fall?

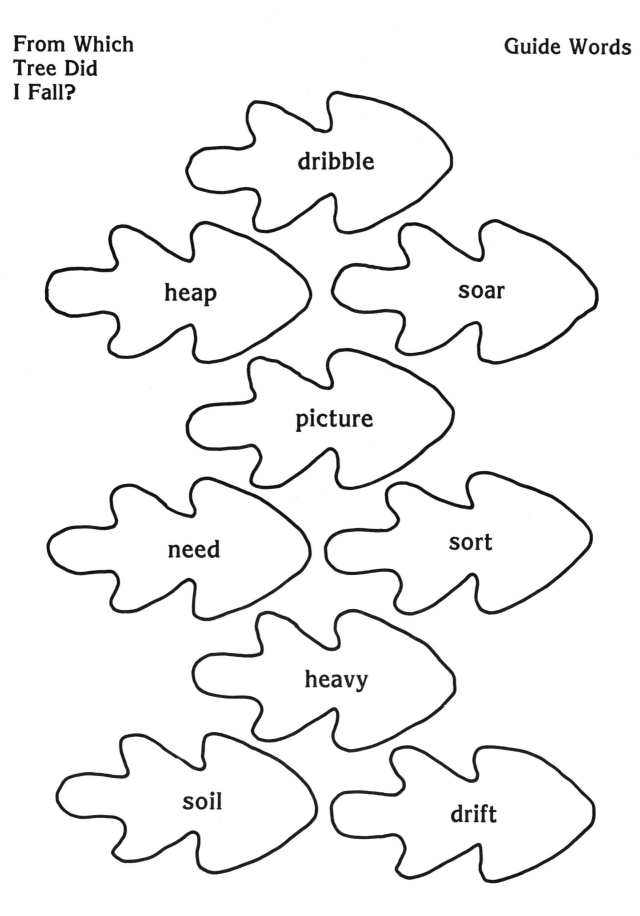

dribble

heap

soar

picture

need

sort

heavy

soil

drift

Call Number Recognition

From Which Tree Did I Fall?

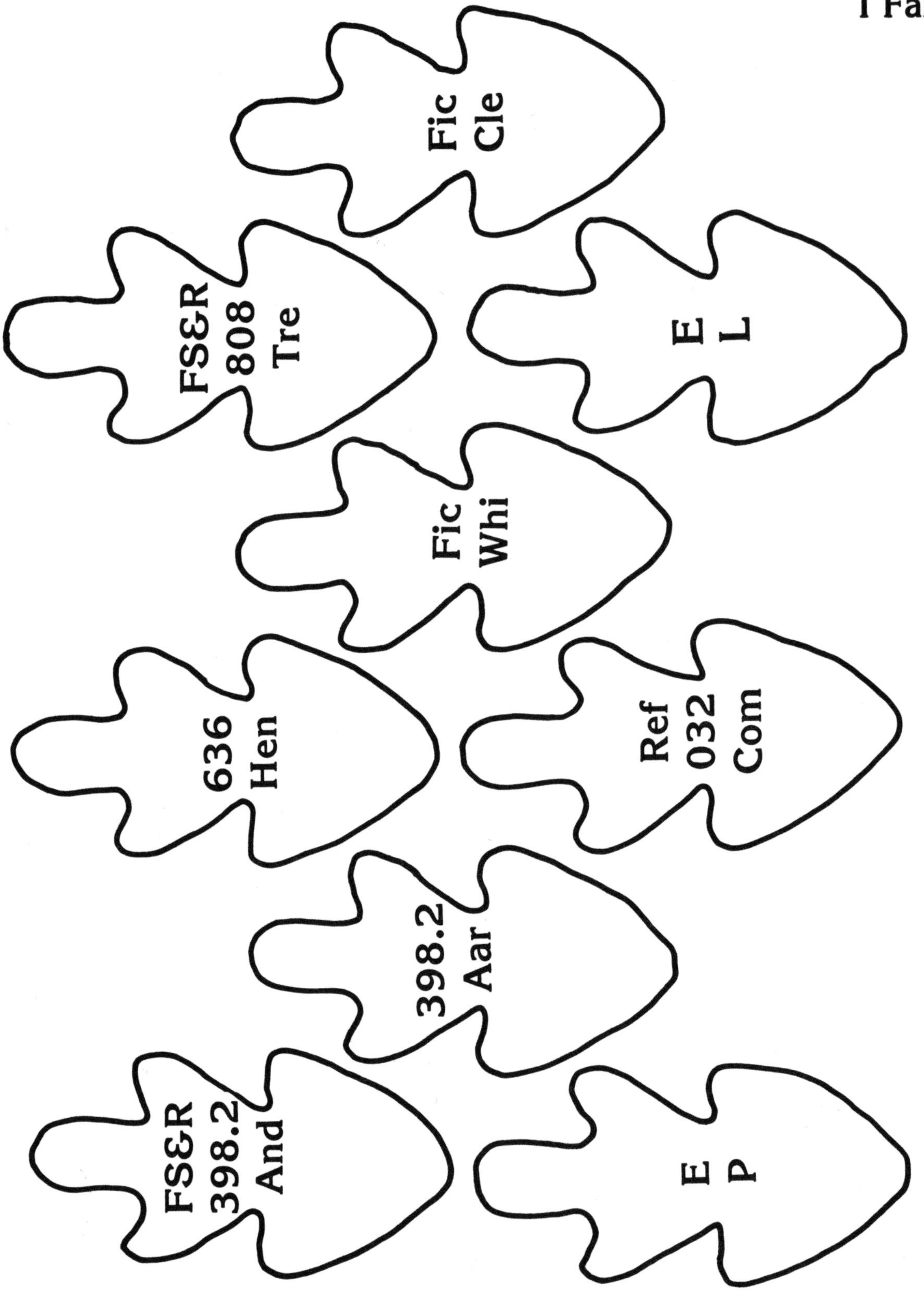
Fic Cle
FS&R 808 Tre
E L
Fic Whi
636 Hen
Ref 032 Com
398.2 Aar
FS&R 398.2 And
E P

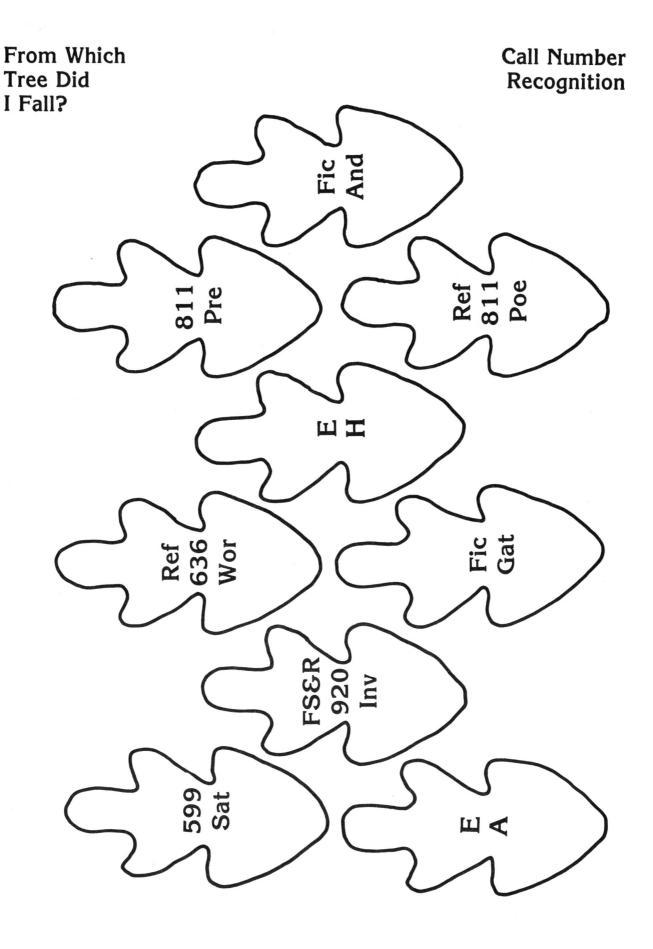

Call Number Recognition

From Which Tree Did I Fall?

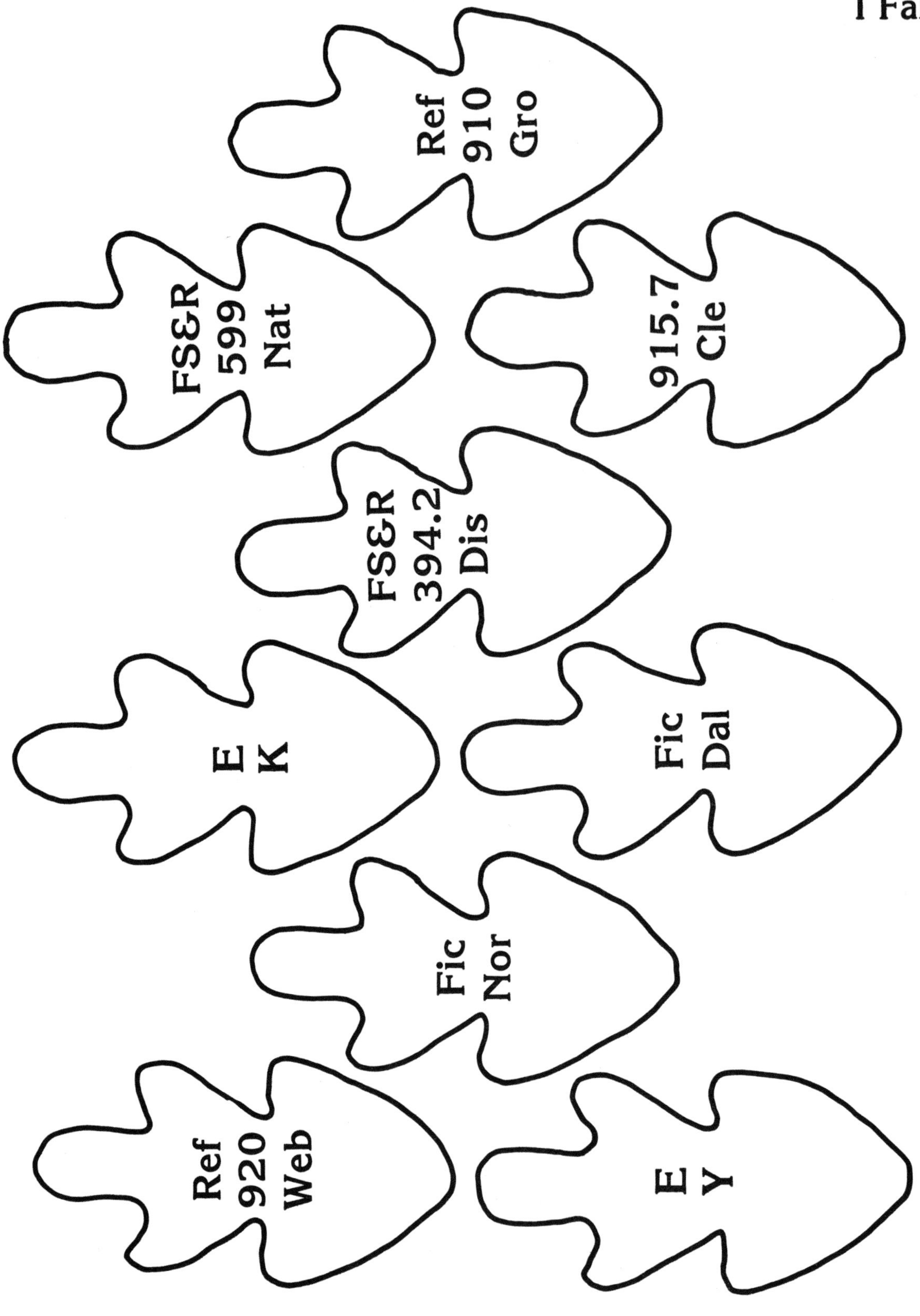

Ref 910 Gro
FS&R 599 Nat
915.7 Cle
FS&R 394.2 Dis
E K
Fic Dal
Fic Nor
Ref 920 Web
E Y

WHICH VOLUME?

Skill Reinforced

Identifying the correct volume of a reference book

Type of Activity

Whole class game
Center (see Follow-up Activities)

Grade Level: 2–4

Time Required

One session

Prerequisite

Guide word practice

Materials

Transparency of volume list
Which Volume? game cards

Procedure

1. Project transparency so that all can see.
2. Shuffle Which Volume? cards and distribute one to each child.
3. One student reads the word aloud and tells which volume to use to look up the word. If the answer is correct, go on to the next student. If the answer is incorrect, have the class help the child and give the student a new card; come back after finishing the class to let this student have another try with a new word. Every child should be able to answer correctly at least once.

Follow-up Activities

ENCYCLOPEDIA SEARCH
Make a center activity by mounting a copy of the volume list on construction paper. Students may pick ten words from the game cards and write the words on the answer sheet. The students then use the volume list to determine which volume is correct.

WHICH VOLUME?

Name _____

WORD	VOLUME NUMBER	WORD	VOLUME NUMBER
1. _____	_____	6. _____	_____
2. _____	_____	7. _____	_____
3. _____	_____	8. _____	_____
4. _____	_____	9. _____	_____
5. _____	_____	10. _____	_____

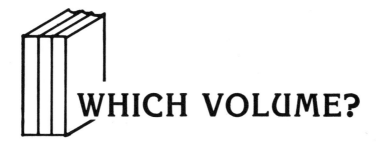

WHICH VOLUME?

1. ABALONE—BIRTHDAY
2. BISON—CRANEFLY
3. CRIME—FRANCE
4. FRANKLIN—JADE
5. JAGUAR—MOCKINGBIRD
6. MODERN ART—PLAY
7. POETRY—SHIP
8. SHRIMP—TURTLES
9. TWAIN—INDEX

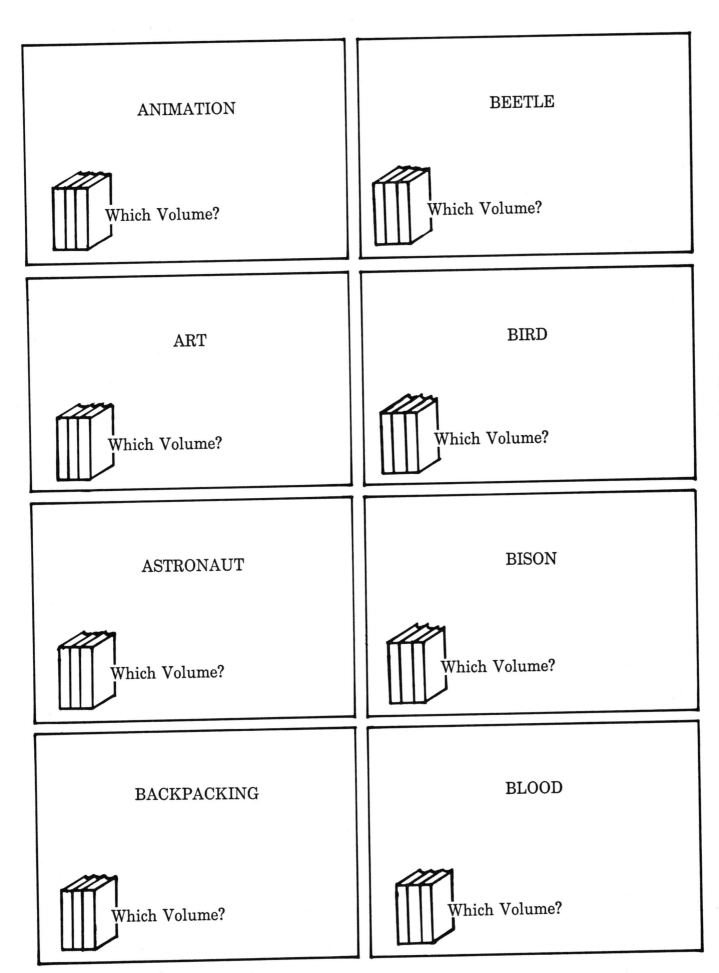

ANIMATION

Which Volume?

BEETLE

Which Volume?

ART

Which Volume?

BIRD

Which Volume?

ASTRONAUT

Which Volume?

BISON

Which Volume?

BACKPACKING

Which Volume?

BLOOD

Which Volume?

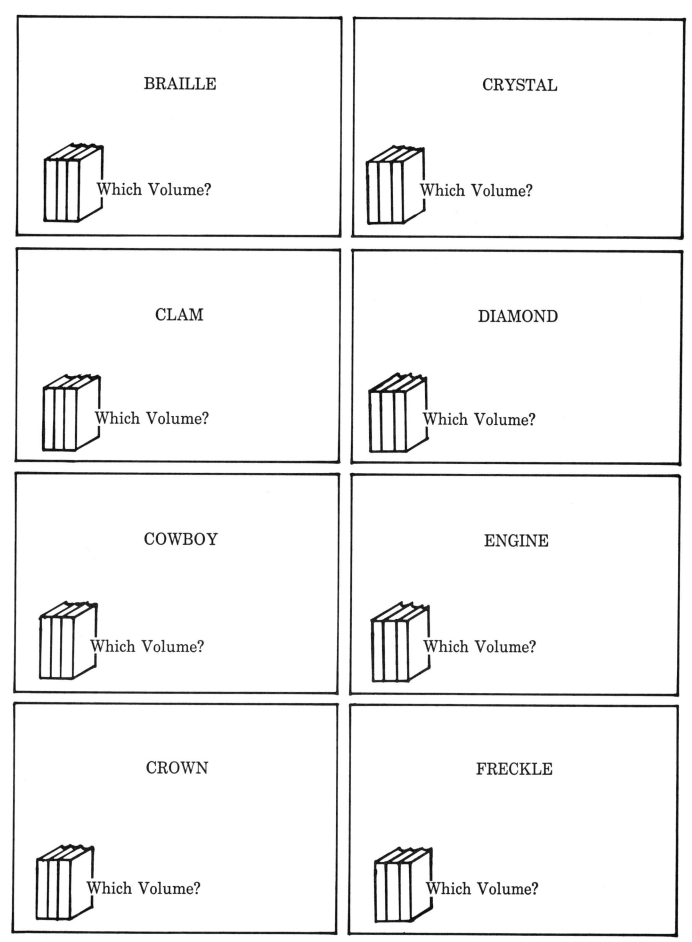

BRAILLE

Which Volume?

CRYSTAL

Which Volume?

CLAM

Which Volume?

DIAMOND

Which Volume?

COWBOY

Which Volume?

ENGINE

Which Volume?

CROWN

Which Volume?

FRECKLE

Which Volume?

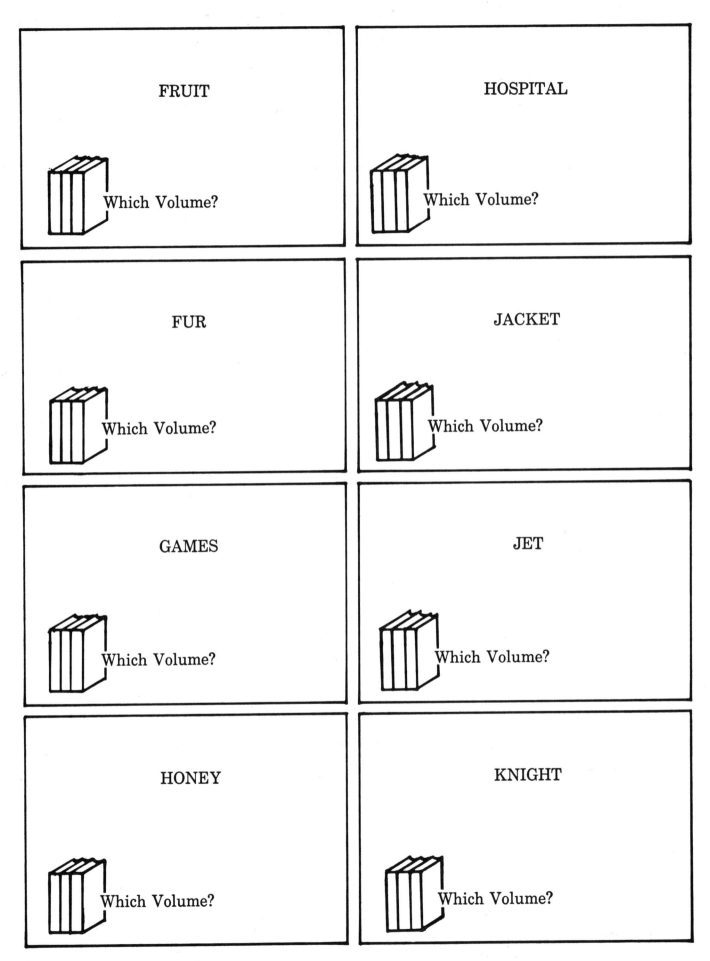

FRUIT

Which Volume?

HOSPITAL

Which Volume?

FUR

Which Volume?

JACKET

Which Volume?

GAMES

Which Volume?

JET

Which Volume?

HONEY

Which Volume?

KNIGHT

Which Volume?

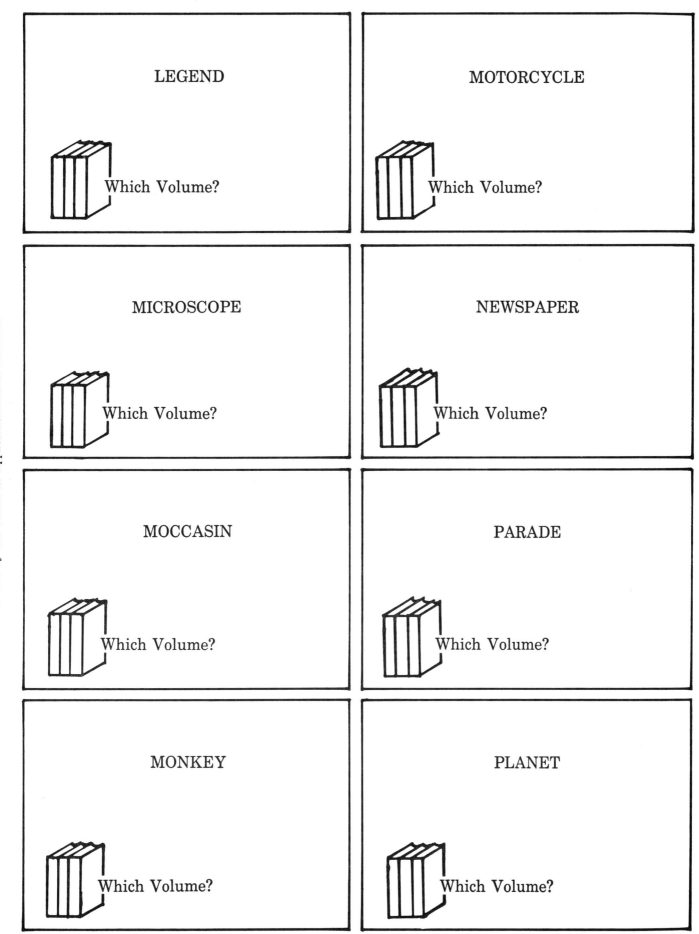

LEGEND

Which Volume?

MOTORCYCLE

Which Volume?

MICROSCOPE

Which Volume?

NEWSPAPER

Which Volume?

MOCCASIN

Which Volume?

PARADE

Which Volume?

MONKEY

Which Volume?

PLANET

Which Volume?

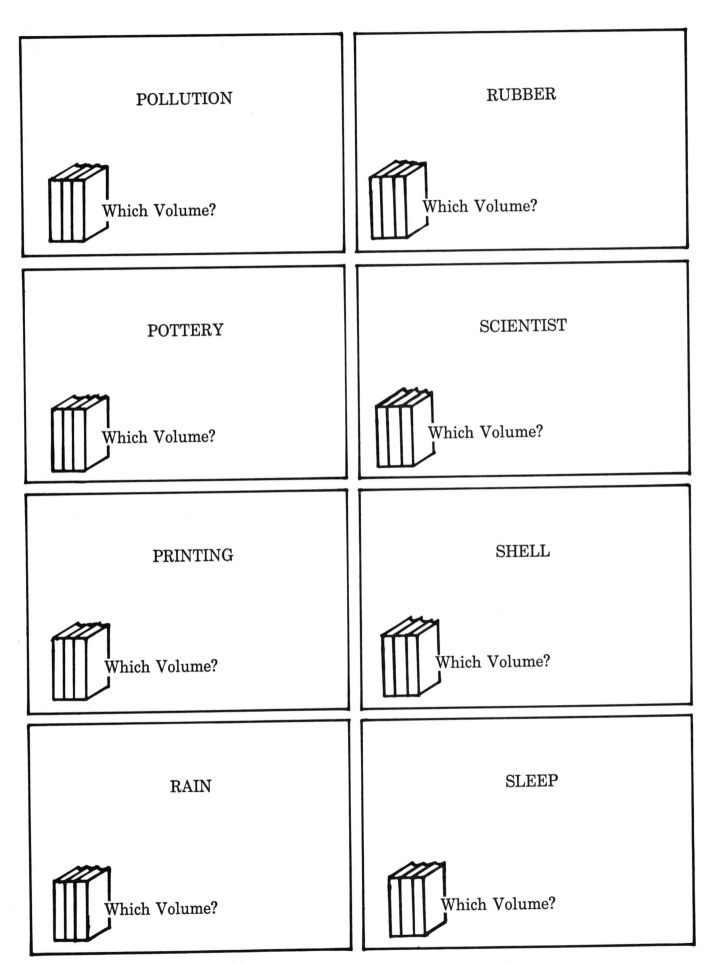

POLLUTION

Which Volume?

RUBBER

Which Volume?

POTTERY

Which Volume?

SCIENTIST

Which Volume?

PRINTING

Which Volume?

SHELL

Which Volume?

RAIN

Which Volume?

SLEEP

Which Volume?

SPY Which Volume?	TIME Which Volume?
STAMP Which Volume?	TOY Which Volume?
SUBWAY Which Volume?	UFO Which Volume?
SUGAR Which Volume?	YAK Which Volume?

CARD CATALOG SEARCH

Skill Reinforced

Using the card catalog to find subjects and appropriate nonfiction call numbers

Type of Activity

Whole class game

Grade Level: 2+

Time Required

Two sessions minimum

Prerequisite

Introduction to card catalog and call numbers

Materials

Search cards
Card Catalog Search answer sheets

Procedure

1. Let students work in pairs or in groups of three.
2. Distribute an answer sheet and one subject card per group. (Be sure not to give two cards for the same catalog drawer.)
3. The group records the subject on the answer sheet and looks it up in the card catalog.
4. Students then record the top line of a nonfiction call number for that subject on the answer sheet.
5. The teacher approves the answer and exchanges the subject card for a new one.
6. Students continue until time is up or until each group has done at least five subjects.

Notes: The slowest groups should find at least two subjects in a half hour. Better students will get more practice. Remind students that it is not just the quantity that counts—it is understanding the process!

With the possibility of all the drawers of the card catalog out at one time, it is helpful to mark the drawers and the frame of the card catalog so drawers can be put back properly.

Variation

This can also be used as a center activity. A student selects a number of subject cards and records the subjects on an answer sheet. The student then goes to the media center and uses the card catalog to find the call numbers.

Follow-up Activity

WHAT'S MY POSITION?

CARD CATALOG SEARCH

Name _____

Subject	Call Number
1.	
2.	
3.	
4.	
5.	
6.	
7.	
8.	
9.	
10.	

CARD CATALOG SEARCH

Name _____

Subject	Call Number
1.	
2.	
3.	
4.	
5.	
6.	
7.	
8.	
9.	
10.	

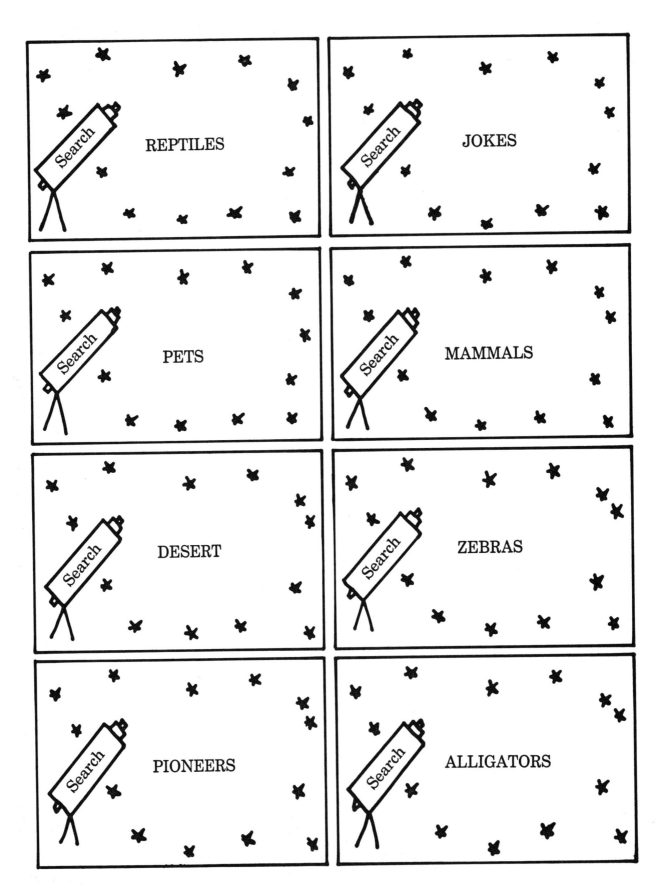

REPTILES

JOKES

PETS

MAMMALS

DESERT

ZEBRAS

PIONEERS

ALLIGATORS

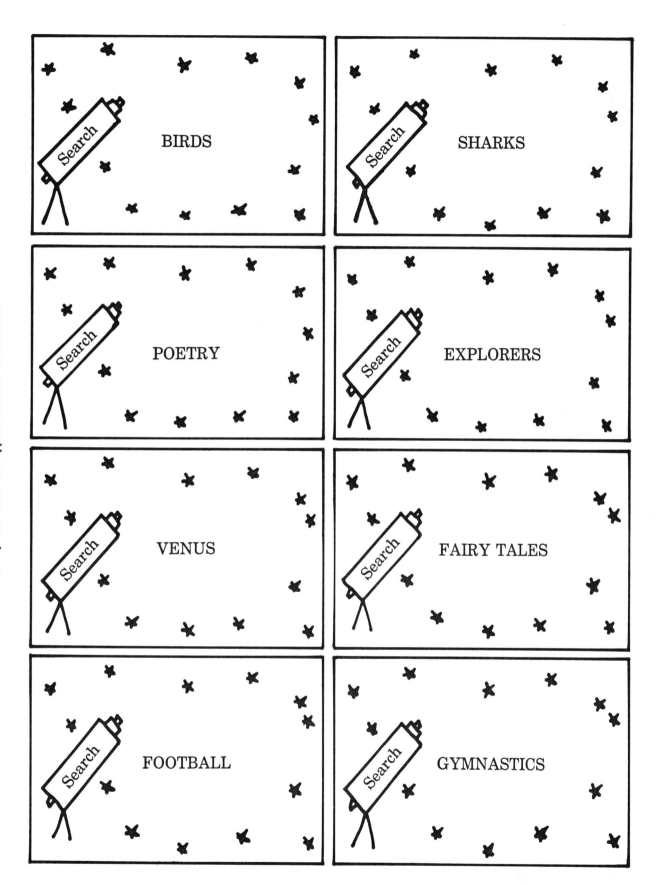

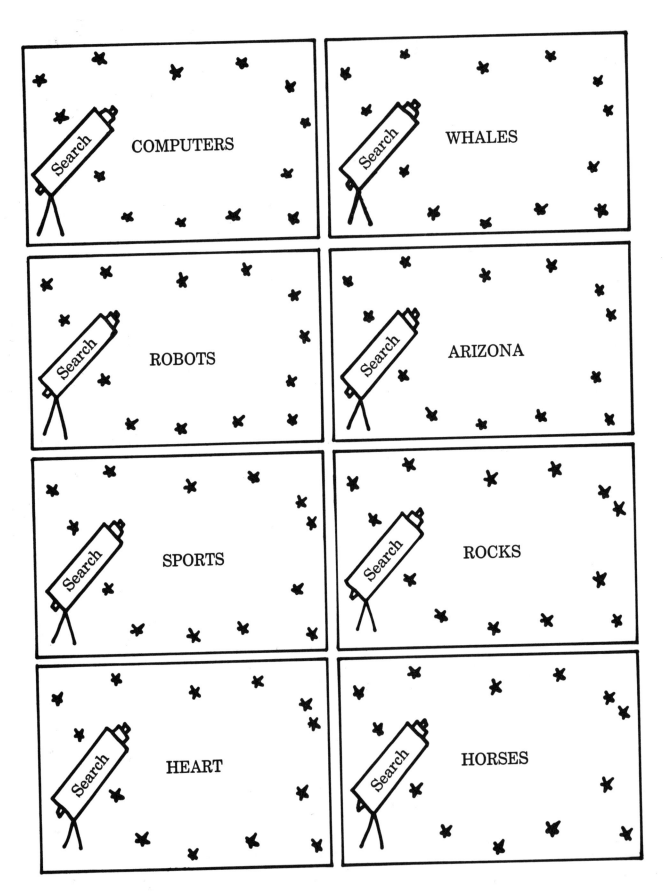

COMPUTERS

WHALES

ROBOTS

ARIZONA

SPORTS

ROCKS

HEART

HORSES

Search

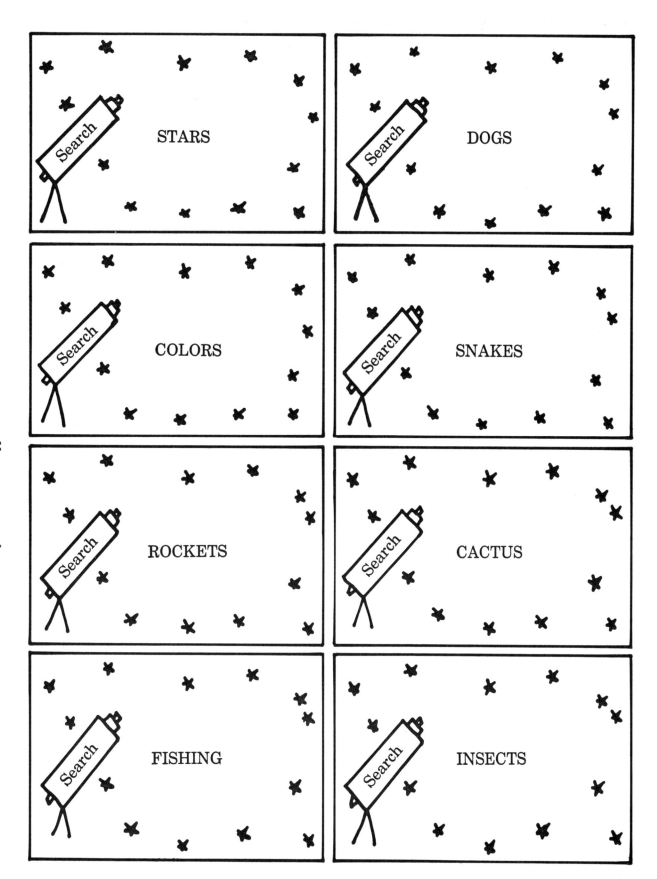

STARS

DOGS

COLORS

SNAKES

ROCKETS

CACTUS

FISHING

INSECTS

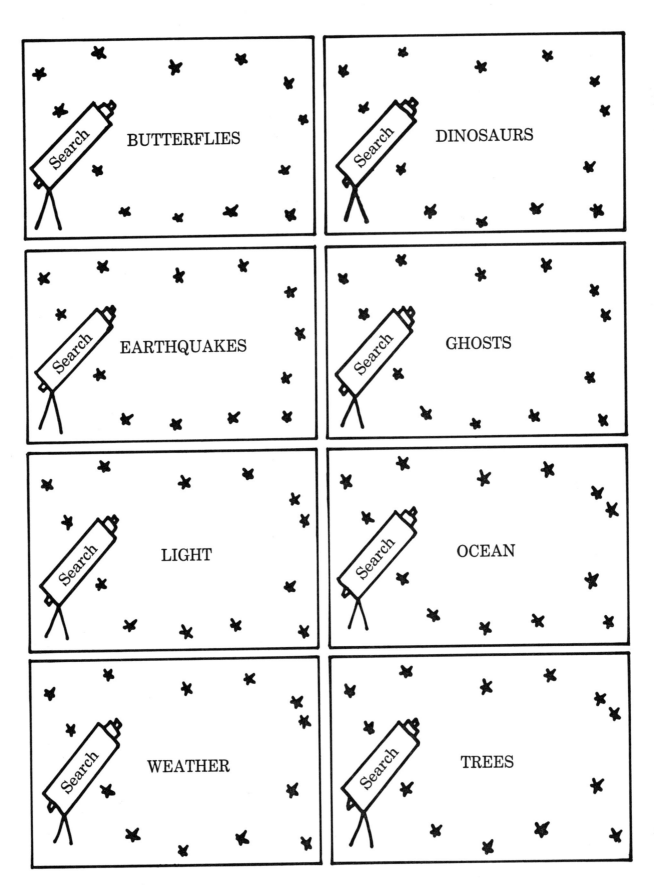

BUTTERFLIES

DINOSAURS

EARTHQUAKES

GHOSTS

LIGHT

OCEAN

WEATHER

TREES

ENCYCLOPEDIA SEARCH

Skills Reinforced

Looking up subjects in encyclopedias
Recording bibliographic information

Type of Activity

Partners
Paper and pencil

Grade Level: 2–4

Time Required

One session

Prerequisites

WHICH VOLUME?
AM I IN THIS VOLUME? (CHOOSE AND CHECK)

Materials

Search cards (see CARD CATALOG SEARCH)
Encyclopedia Search answer sheets
Pencils

Procedure

1. Divide class into pairs.
2. Distribute an Encyclopedia Search answer sheet and a search card to each pair.
3. Students are to look up the subject on the search card in an encyclopedia.
4. Have students record the entry wording used in the encyclopedia, along with the title of the set, the volume number, and the page numbers.

Note: Students should not write down the subject on the answer sheet before looking it up; sometimes the entry word used in the encyclopedia will not exactly match the subject written on the card.

Variation

Have students look up one article using a search card. Then have them look up four additional articles that relate to that topic. For example, suppose they first looked up *bears* and recorded the information on line 1; they might look up *hibernation, mammals, polar bears,* and *honey* for 2 through 5.

Follow-up Activities

RECORD THAT SOURCE!
Have students pick one of the subjects and take some notes about it (see LET YOUR KNOWLEDGE BLOSSOM).

ENCYCLOPEDIA SEARCH

Name _____

ENTRY	TITLE	VOLUME	PAGE
1.			
2.			
3.			
4.			
5.			

ENCYCLOPEDIA SEARCH

Name _____

ENTRY	TITLE	VOLUME	PAGE
1.			
2.			
3.			
4.			
5.			

AN OCEAN OF WORDS

Skills Reinforced

Vocabulary development
Using a thesaurus

Type of Activity

Individuals or partners
Paper and pencil or center

Grade Level: 3–6

Time Required

Varies with number of worksheets used

Materials

One or more of the following worksheets reproduced in appropriate quantities:
The Beach Walk
The Golden Eggs
The Fox and the Grapes
The Milkmaid and Her Pail
Crossword Puzzle 1
Crossword Puzzle 2
The Clear and Simple Thesaurus Dictionary (Grosset & Dunlap, 1971).

Story Worksheet Directions

1. Students can work alone or in pairs. While it is ideal to have a classroom set of thesauri, this activity can be completed with one thesaurus set up in a center in the classroom or media center.

2. Students use the thesaurus to find appropriate synonyms for the capitalized words in the stories.

3. Share the stories with the whole class as everyone comes up with different possibilities.

Crossword Puzzle Directions

Students use the thesaurus to find synonyms that fit the number of spaces and letter match the other words that cross it. Answers for both puzzles are included.

Variation

Other stories and crossword puzzles could be designed by teachers or students for any subject area.

Note: A different thesaurus could be used; however, it would need to be checked to see if it contains the capitalized words in the stories.

ANSWERS FOR CROSSWORDS

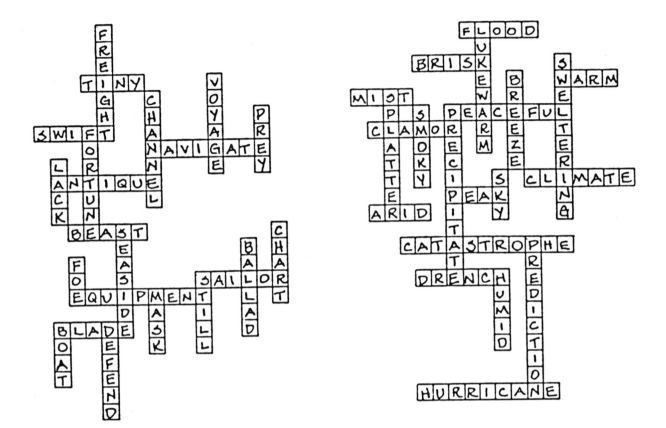

THESAURUS WORKSHEET

Name _____ Room number _____

Fill in the blanks by finding appropriate synonyms for the words in CAPITAL letters.
Be sure to use the thesaurus and watch for plurals and the past tense.

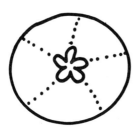

The Beach Walk

One day I walked out to the WHARF _____ . I looked out across

the ocean and THOUGHT _____ I saw a whale, but it was a

SEAL _____ . I had started along the BEACH _____

when I spied a MICROSCOPIC _____ piece of red. I kicked at it with

my foot; it HIT _____ something firm. There must be something

CONCEALED _____ ! I QUICKLY _____ started to DIG

_____ in the sand. I finally pulled out an ANCIENT _____

BLADE _____ . I wondered if I should dig some more; maybe there was a

TREASURE _____ under my feet. All of a sudden I felt something MOIST

_____ grab my foot! It was just some SUCCULENT _____

seaweed that had ATTACKED _____ me. By now I was thirsty but

there was only the salty water to DRINK _____ . Next time I make an

EXPEDITION _____ I should remember to bring some kind of

NUTRITION _____ with me. I DECIDED _____ to head

for home; I wish I could have taken photographs of today's ADVENTURES

_____ .

THESAURUS WORKSHEET

Name _____ Room number _____

Fill in the blanks by finding appropriate synonyms for the words in CAPITAL letters. Be sure to use the thesaurus and watch for correct meanings, plurals, and the past tense.

The Golden Eggs

One day a farmer went to the nest of his goose to see if she had LAID

_____ an egg. To his surprise, he FOUND _____ , instead

of an ORDINARY _____ goose egg, an egg of SOLID

_____ gold.

"What a FINE _____ goose!" he cried. "I can SELL _____

this egg for a GREAT DEAL _____ of MONEY _____ ."

EVERY _____ morning after that the farmer found another golden

EGG _____ in the nest. Every day he sold the golden egg. He was slowly

GROWING _____ RICH _____ .

But as the farmer grew rich, he grew greedy. One day he SAID _____

to himself, "My goose lays ONLY _____ one golden egg each day. NO

DOUBT_____ there are MANY _____ more inside her!"

And he had no REST _____ until he had KILLED _____

the goose.

"Oh me, oh my!" said the farmer. "Why was I so greedy? Now I shall be POOR

_____ again. I have killed the goose that laid the

GOLDEN _____ eggs!"

© 1990 by The Center for Applied Research in Education

THESAURUS WORKSHEET

Name _____ Room number _____

Fill in the blanks by finding appropriate synonyms for the words in CAPITAL letters. Be sure to use the thesaurus and watch for plurals and the past tense.

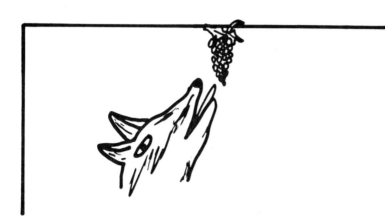

The Fox and the Grapes

One WARM _____ day a fox was SLINKING _____

through the WOODS _____ . NOW _____ the fox was

very THIRSTY, _____ and when he saw some DELICIOUS _____

grapes HANGING _____ in a cluster high on a vine, he felt he MUST

_____ have them.

He JUMPED _____ and he JUMPED _____ , but he

could not JUMP _____ high ENOUGH _____ to REACH

_____ the grapes. At last he grew TIRED _____ of

trying and went off MUTTERING _____ to himself, "The grapes are

probably SOUR _____ , anyway."

Sometimes PEOPLE _____ are just as SILLY _____ as

that fox: When they cannot get what they WANT _____ , they make

believe there is something WRONG _____ with it.

THESAURUS WORKSHEET

Name _____ Room number _____

Fill in the blanks by finding appropriate synonyms for the words in CAPITAL letters.
Be sure to use the thesaurus and watch for plurals and the past tense.

 *The Milkmaid and Her Pail*

A milkmaid was on her way to MARKET _____ , CARRYING

_____ a pail of milk on the TOP _____ of her head. As

she WALKED _____ along the ROAD _____ in the

WARM _____ sunshine, she began to THINK _____ of all

the things she would BUY _____ with the MONEY _____

she was going to RECEIVE _____ for the milk.

"I will buy some hens," she told herself, "and they will lay eggs EVERY

_____ day. Then I will SELL _____ the eggs at the

market, and with the money I will buy myself a NEW _____ green dress

with a green ribbon. Then I will GO _____ to the fair. All the YOUNG

_____ men will want to be my dancing PARTNER _____ ,

but I will TOSS _____ my curls and say 'no' to every one of them."

As she spoke, the milkmaid TRIPPED _____ on a STONE

_____ . Down came the PAIL _____ of milk, spilling over

the GROUND _____ . Nothing was left but an empty pail and the

SCOLDING _____ she would receive when she returned home.

"That," she said to herself as she lay on the ground, "will TEACH _____

me not to COUNT _____ my chickens before they are hatched!"

© 1990 by The Center for Applied Research in Education

Name _____ Room number _____

THESAURUS SKILLS

CROSSWORD PUZZLE 1

Use the thesaurus to find synonyms that fit the number of spaces and match letters with other words.

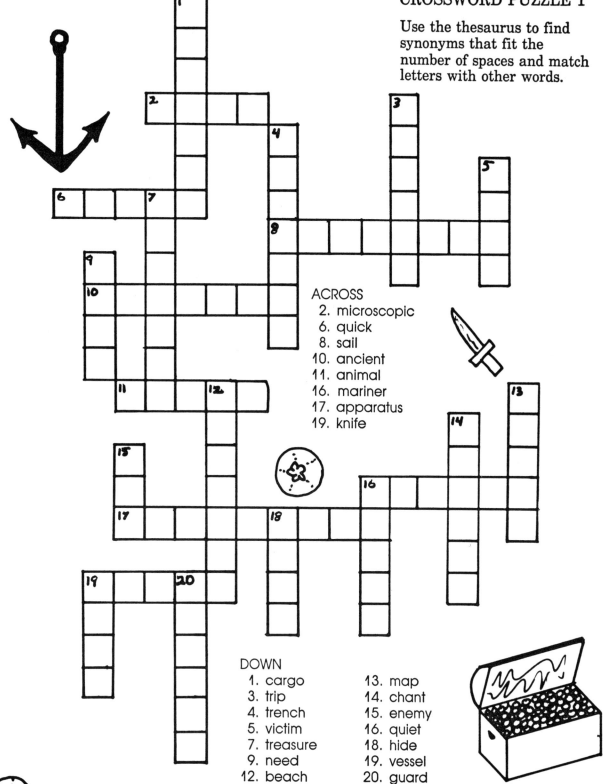

ACROSS
2. microscopic
6. quick
8. sail
10. ancient
11. animal
16. mariner
17. apparatus
19. knife

DOWN
1. cargo
3. trip
4. trench
5. victim
7. treasure
9. need
12. beach

13. map
14. chant
15. enemy
16. quiet
18. hide
19. vessel
20. guard

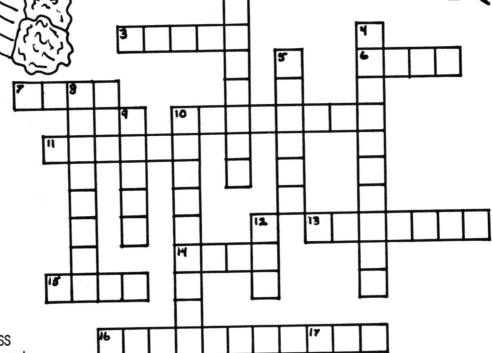

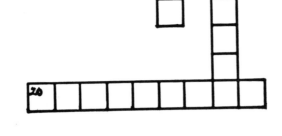

THESAURUS SKILLS

CROSSWORD PUZZLE 2

Use the thesaurus to find synonyms that fit the number of spaces and match letters with other words.

ACROSS
1. torrent
3. chilly
6. heat
7. vapor
10. tranquil
11. roar
13. weather
14. zenith
15. dry
16. disaster
18. soak
20. typhoon

DOWN
2. tepid
4. torrid
5. wind
8. splash
9. hazy
10. rain
12. heaven
17. forecast
19. muggy

DESIGN MAGIC

Skill Reinforced

Using map coordinates

Type of Activity

Whole class art
Center

Grade Level: 3+

Time Required

Two or three sessions

Materials

Overhead projector
What's My Location? transparency
Design Magic Samples 1 and 2 (made into transparencies)
Colored markers for transparencies
Design Magic worksheets, reproduced for each student
Crayons

Procedure

1. Review the concept of coordinates by showing the What's My Location? transparency.
2. Ask the students many questions about the shapes and their locations. For example, what is in C4?; what is in F6 and F7?; where is the bee? (D6).
3. After locating all the shapes, students could be asked to come up and make other shapes in other available spaces on the grid. A good way to involve more students is to have one student decide on the shape, another state the coordinates, and a third make the simple drawing.
4. Show the Design Magic Sample 1 transparency.
5. One by one, let students come up and color in a square as directed by the coordinates at the bottom of the page. Be sure students color in the WHOLE square.
6. Point out that the finished picture looks boxy but the rainbow still shows.
7. Show the Design Magic Sample 2 transparency.
8. The students will need to identify the colors using the code squares at the side or the teacher can color in the boxes on the sample.
9. Fill in the coordinates for each color of the jack-o'-lantern at the bottom of the transparency.
10. Distribute the Design Magic worksheets and let students design their own pictures.

Variations

- Have students draw pictures of many objects or collect pictures from magazines. Cover a bulletin board with butcher paper. Draw a grid onto the paper. Let the students tack or tape their pictures onto the paper.
- Then one student asks a question about the location of a picture; the rest of the class finds it and tells its location.

- Students can use regular graph paper for their pictures. They should make a star in the very first full square on the top left of the graph paper, write letters of the alphabet (one letter per square) down the paper from the star, and write numbers consecutively across the paper from the star (see the worksheets).
- Worksheets may be placed in a center.

Follow-up Activities

Show a variety of atlases to the students. *Hammond Large Type World Atlas* is a good resource because the maps are large and simple enough for use with a full class. Pick an interesting or known city or landmark. Use the index and coordinates to show the students that they can find the location.

PRESIDENTIAL CITIES IN THE U.S.A.

What's My Location?

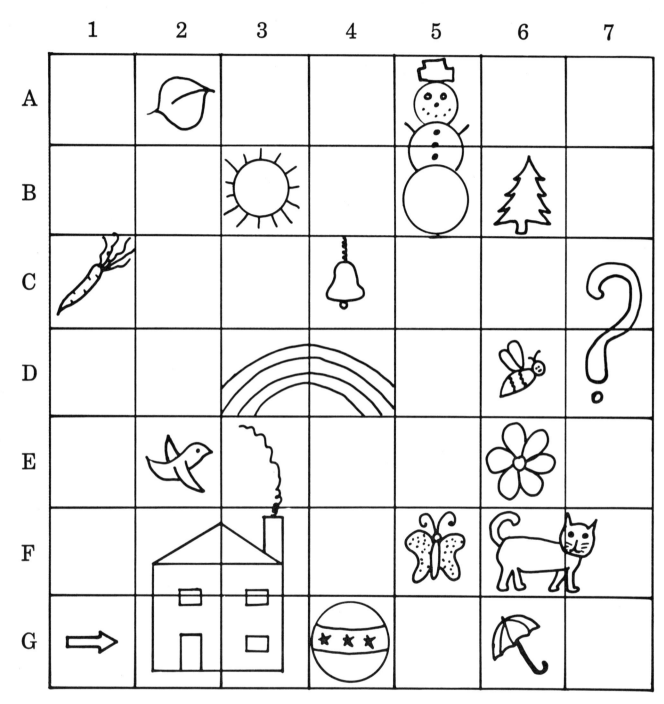

Design Magic Sample 1

Color the picture using the coordinates below.

★	1	2	3	4	5	6	7	8	9	10	11	12
A												
B												
C												
D												
E												
F												
G												
H												
I												
J												
K												
L												

YELLOW
D-4–9
E-3–10
F-2, 3, 10, 11
G-1, 2, 11, 12
H-1, 12

GREEN
F-4–9
G-3, 4, 9, 10
H-2, 3, 10, 11
I-1, 2, 11, 12
J-1, 12

BLUE
G-5–8
H-4–9
I-3, 4, 9, 10
J-2, 3, 10, 11
K-1, 2, 11, 12
L-1, 12

RED
B-3–9
C-2–10
D-2, 3, 10, 11
E-1, 2, 11, 12

PURPLE
I-5–8
J-4, 9
K-3, 10
L-2, 11

Design Magic Sample 2

Write the coordinates for this picture.

	orange
	brown
	black

ORANGE
A-
B-
C-
D-
E-
F-
G-
H-
I-
J-
K-
L-

BROWN
A-
B-
C-
D-
E-
F-
G-
H-
I-
J-
K-
L-

BLACK
A-
B-
C-
D-
E-
F-
G-
H-
I-
J-
K-
L-

Design Magic Worksheet

Draw your picture on the grid to the right. Remember, only one color can be used in each square.

Write the coordinates for each color in the chart below.

Copy your coordinates onto another paper. See if a friend can draw your picture!

★	1	2	3	4	5	6	7	8	9	10	11	12
A												
B												
C												
D												
E												
F												
G												
H												
I												
J												
K												
L												

YELLOW	GREEN	BLUE	RED	ORANGE	PURPLE	BROWN	BLACK
A-	A-	A-	A-	A-	A-	A-	A-
B-	B-	B-	B-	B-	B-	B-	B-
C-	C-	C-	C-	C-	C-	C-	C-
D-	D-	D-	D-	D-	D-	D-	D-
E-	E-	E-	E-	E-	E-	E-	E-
F-	F-	F-	F-	F-	F-	F-	F-
G-	G-	G-	G-	G-	G-	G-	G-
H-	H-	H-	H-	H-	H-	H-	H-
I-	I-	I-	I-	I-	I-	I-	I-
J-	J-	J-	J-	J-	J-	J-	J-
K-	K-	K-	K-	K-	K-	K-	K-
L-	L-	L-	L-	L-	L-	L-	L-

PRESIDENTIAL CITIES IN THE U.S.A.

Skill Reinforced

Using an atlas

Type of Activity

Whole class or center depending on the number of atlases available
Paper and pencil

Grade Level: 4+

Time Required

One session

Prerequisite

DESIGN MAGIC

Materials

Atlas
PRESIDENTIAL CITIES IN THE U.S.A. worksheet

Procedure

1. Distribute worksheets to each student.
2. Using the gazeteer in the atlas, students identify which town listed on the worksheet goes with which state.
3. They look up the towns on the maps in the atlas.
4. They identify the outline of the state on the worksheet and make a dot showing the approximate location of the town.
5. Each town and state should be correctly labeled.

Variations

Use animals or native American tribal names for a theme. Have students create their own worksheets by identifying the cities and towns that fit the theme (Salmon, Idaho and Buffalo, New York or Oshkosh, Wisconsin, Sioux City, Iowa, and Navajo, New Mexico). To make a worksheet students draw the outline shape of the appropriate states and list the names of the cities and states.

Answers

See illustration.

Name _____ Room number _____

PRESENTIAL CITIES
IN THE U.S.A.

Match each town with
the state it is in,
placing a dot to
show its location.

Arthur
Cleveland
Coolidge
Fillmore
Jackson
Lincoln
Madison
Taft
Washington

STATES

Arizona
California
Florida
Georgia
Illinois
Nebraska
Ohio
Wisconsin
Wyoming

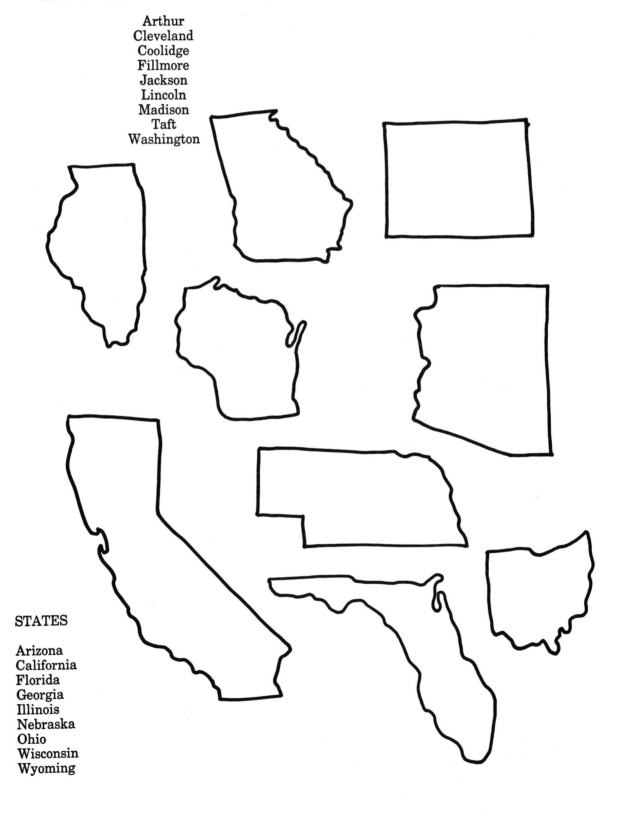

UNDERSTANDING THE RESEARCH PROCESS

RIBBIT

Skills Reinforced

Listening
Understanding the purpose of research

Type of Activity

Whole class movement

Grade Level: 3–5

Time Required

One session

Prerequisite

None

Materials

Transparency of Ribbit Chorus
Ribbit Cue-You cards, reproduced and cut apart
Dialogue for Ribbit Cue-You
Ribbit bookmarks, reproduced onto green cardstock, cut out, and laminated if desired

Procedure

1. Introduce the activity by asking children what a frog says. Accept all answers and then tell them that in this story the frog says, "Ribbit," and that today's activity will explain to them what ribbit means.

2. Shuffle Ribbit Cue-You cards and distribute to the students. Most likely there will be extra cards; some children may have two.

3. Tell the students that they are to listen for someone to say the "cue" line on the card; then they are to say the "you" line.

4. Show the transparency of the chorus and have students read it in unison. Inform the students that they will be reading the chorus twice in the story and they will have to listen for a classmate to say something to the effect of "Let's sing our song!" so they will know when to come in. (All students should say the chorus; it is not written on a Cue-You card.)

5. When everyone thinks they understand the procedure and can read all the words on their cards, the teacher says, "Someone has the cue, 'When the class is quiet, you begin.' "

6. The teacher can follow along with the dialogue sheet while students tell the story.

7. After the game write "R I B B I T" vertically on the board. As a review ask students to tell you what each letter represents and to write the answers on the board.

8. Hand out Ribbit bookmarks to remind students of the activity.

9. Play the game as often as you and students want or need to reinforce concepts.

Variation

Make a bulletin board (see sample) with a big frog saying "Ribbit" and a group of frogs singing the chorus. Students could draw pictures of bugs to pin up. Discussion with students could identify research "bugs" they have, and activities could be developed to get rid of those bugs.

Sample Bulletin Board

DIALOGUE FOR RIBBIT CUE-YOU

—Ribbit. Ribbit.

—Croak.

—Ribbit. Ribbit. Croak.

—What are you croaking about?

—I have to do a research project and I don't know what to do! (wail)

—But research is fun!

—You've got to be kidding!

—Oh yes, it is. You just have to know the right lyrics.

—Hey! Let's sing our song for him.

   Hop right to it and get it done

   Because research is fun, fun, fun!

   Hop right to it and get it done

   Because all you need is in the library!

—And this is how ribbit goes:

—*R.* Research is fun because you can

—*I.* Investigate any subject you want by looking in

—*B.* Books and using other media as well. We have to remember to

—*B.* That's right, be respectful of other people's thoughts so we write a bibliography and then we

—*I.* Incorporate our own thoughts and ideas with what we've learned as we find a way to

—*T.* Tell or share our research with our friends.

—Oh, I see. That isn't so bad.

—Let's see, *R-I-B-B-I-T.*

—I think I have it!

—*R* is for research, which is fun!

—*I* is for investigating.

—That means we explore the subject.

—*B* is for books and other media like filmstrips.

—Movies.

—Human beings.

—And computer databases.

—*B* is for being respectful of other people's ideas.

—That's why we make a bibliography which is a list of sources.

—*I* is for our own ideas that we add to what we've learned.

—And *T* is for somehow telling others about what we have learned.

—I think I've got it! Ribbit! Ribbit! Ribbit!

—That is easy to remember. *R-I-B-B-I-T.*

—Let's all sing the chorus again!

   Hop right to it and get it done

   Because research is fun, fun, fun!

   Hop right to it and get it done

   Because all you need is in the library!

—This is great. I'll never have to croak again now that I know the catchword.

—Ribbit. Ribbit. Ribbit. Ribbit.

—Splash!

RIBBIT CHORUS

HOP RIGHT TO IT
AND GET IT DONE
BECAUSE RESEARCH IS
FUN, FUN, FUN!

HOP RIGHT TO IT
AND GET IT DONE
BECAUSE ALL YOU NEED
IS IN THE LIBRARY!

CUE: "Oh yes, it is. You just have to know the right lyrics."

YOU: Stand and say, "Hey! Let's sing our song for him." Then the whole class sings the chorus.

CUE: "I. Investigate any subject you want by looking in..."

YOU: Stand and say, "B. Books and using other media as well. We have to remember to..."

CUE: Someone says, "Hey! Let's sing our song for him." And the class sings the chorus.

YOU: Stand and say, "And this is how ribbit goes:"

CUE: "B. Books and using other media as well. We have to remember to..."

YOU: Stand and say, "B. That's right, be respectful of other people's thoughts so we write a bibliography and then we..."

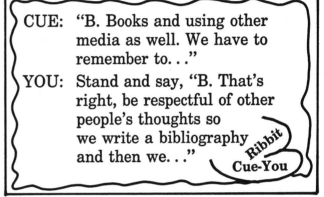

CUE: "And this is how ribbit goes:"

YOU: Stand and say, "R. Research is fun because you can..."

CUE: "B. That's right, be respectful of other people's thoughts so we write a bibliography and then we..."

YOU: Stand and say, "I. Incorporate our own thoughts and ideas with what we've learned as we find a way to..."

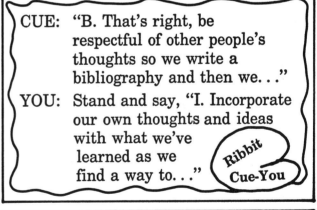

CUE: "R. Research is fun because you can..."

YOU: Stand and say, "I. Investigate any subject you want by looking in..."

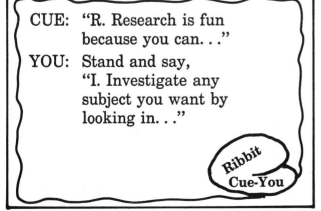

CUE: "I. Incorporate our own thoughts and ideas with what we've learned as we find a way to..."

YOU: Stand and say, "T. Tell or share our research with our friends."

CUE: "T. Tell or share our research with our friends."

YOU: Stand and say, "Oh, I see. That isn't so bad."

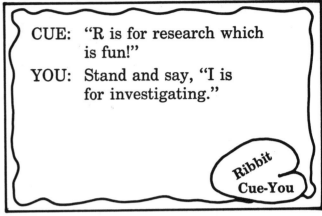

CUE: "R is for research which is fun!"

YOU: Stand and say, "I is for investigating."

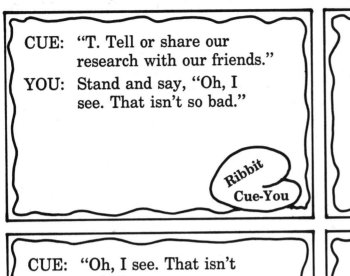

CUE: "Oh, I see. That isn't so bad.

YOU: Stand and say, "Let's see, ribbit. R-I-B-B-I-T."

CUE: "I is for investigating."

YOU: Stand and say, "That means we explore the subject."

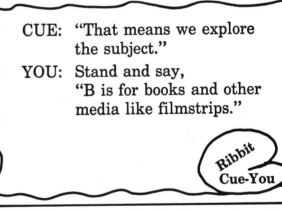

CUE: "Let's see, ribbit. R-I-B-B-I-T."

YOU: Stand and say, "I think I have it."

CUE: "That means we explore the subject."

YOU: Stand and say, "B is for books and other media like filmstrips."

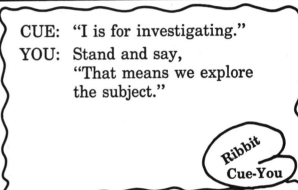

CUE: "I think I have it!"

YOU: Stand and say, "R is for research, which is fun!"

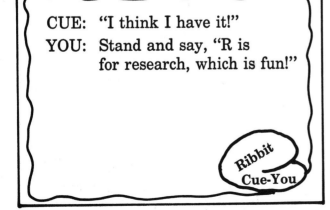

CUE: "B is for books and other media like filmstrips."

YOU: Stand and say, "Movies."

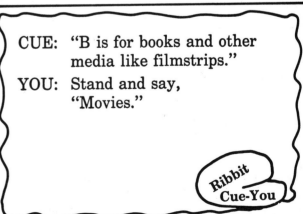

CUE: "Movies."
YOU: Stand and say,
"Human beings."

CUE: "That's why we make a bibliography which is a list of sources."
YOU: Stand and say, "I is for our own ideas that we add to what we've learned."

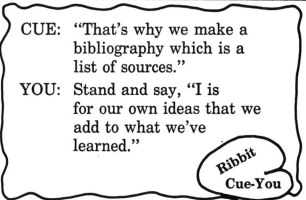

CUE: "Human beings."
YOU: Stand and say,
"And computer databases."

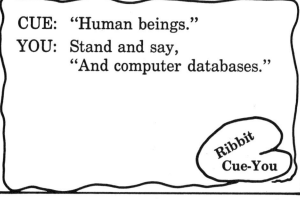

CUE: "I is for our own ideas that we add to what we've learned."
YOU: Stand and say,
"And T is for somehow telling others about what we have learned."

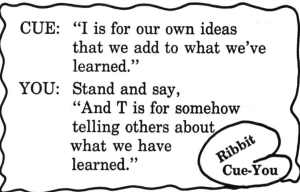

CUE: "And computer databases."
YOU: Stand and say,
"B is for being respectful of other people's ideas."

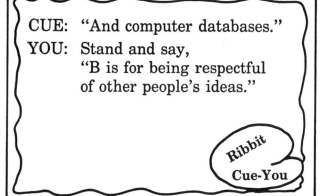

CUE: "And T is for somehow telling others about what we have learned."
YOU: Stand and say,
"I think I've got it! Ribbit! Ribbit! Ribbit!"

CUE: "B is for being respectful of other people's ideas."
YOU: Stand and say,
"That's why we make a bibliography which is a list of sources."

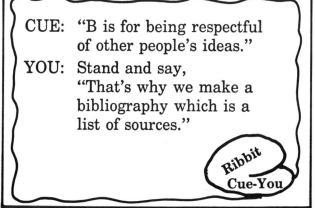

CUE: "I think I've got it! Ribbit! Ribbit! Ribbit!"
YOU: Stand and say, "That is so easy to remember. R-I-B-B-I-T."

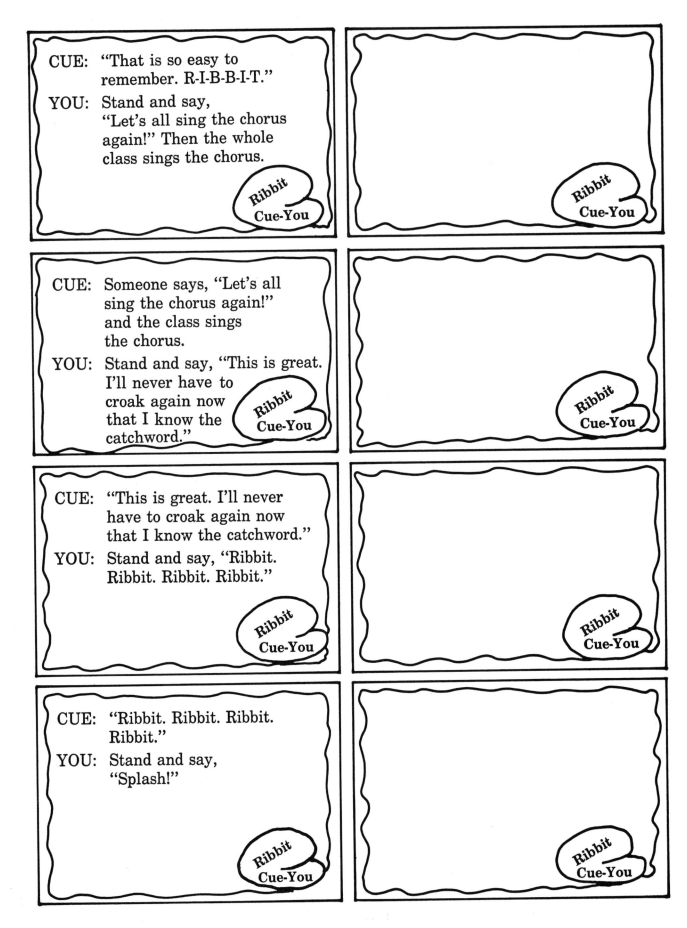

CUE: "That is so easy to remember. R-I-B-B-I-T."

YOU: Stand and say, "Let's all sing the chorus again!" Then the whole class sings the chorus.

Ribbit Cue-You

Ribbit Cue-You

CUE: Someone says, "Let's all sing the chorus again!" and the class sings the chorus.

YOU: Stand and say, "This is great. I'll never have to croak again now that I know the catchword."

Ribbit Cue-You

Ribbit Cue-You

CUE: "This is great. I'll never have to croak again now that I know the catchword."

YOU: Stand and say, "Ribbit. Ribbit. Ribbit. Ribbit."

Ribbit Cue-You

Ribbit Cue-You

CUE: "Ribbit. Ribbit. Ribbit. Ribbit."

YOU: Stand and say, "Splash!"

Ribbit Cue-You

Ribbit Cue-You

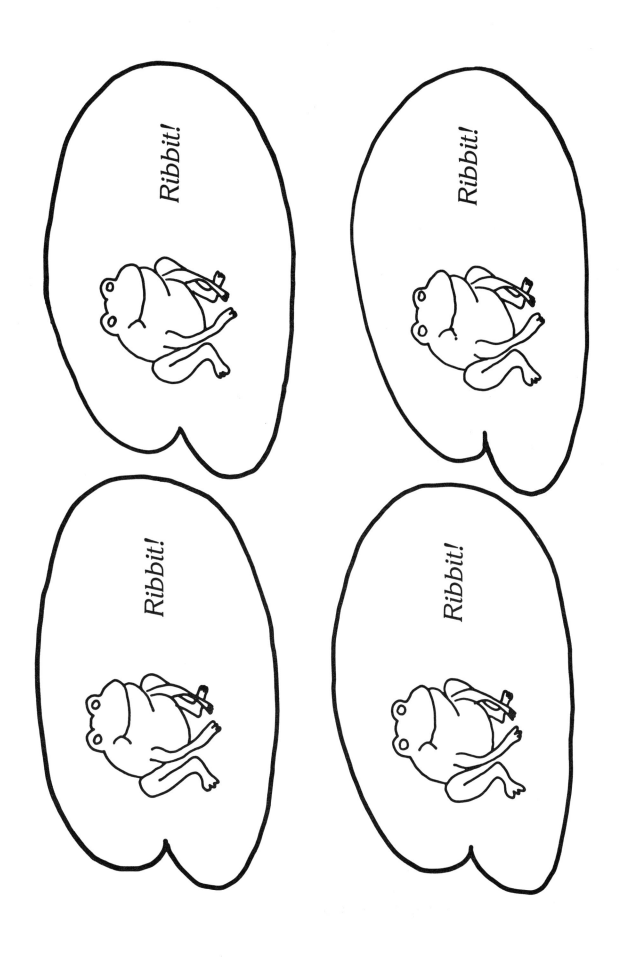

CLIMB MOUNT EVEREST

Skills Reinforced

Understanding the research process

Type of Activity

Whole class or individual art activity
Center

Grade Level: 2–4

Time Required

Several sessions, depending on the activity or activities selected

Prerequisites

Le Grand Tour
Look It Up!
What's My Position?

Materials

Several boot prints cut out of brown paper, grocery bags, or card stock
Snowflake patterns
Four-inch circle pattern
Tent patterns
Radio Message worksheet
Pennant pattern
Paper bags (lunch or grocery size)
Scissors
Crayons, markers, yarn, etc.
Glue

Procedure

Pick the activity or activities students are to work on (e.g., boot prints, puppets, snowballs). Follow the directions for that activity.

Directions for Boot Prints

1. Identify the steps the students will need to go through to complete a research project (see possible steps on next page).
2. Cut out more than enough boot prints to record each step on one plus have some extra in case more steps need to be added.
3. Write each step on a boot print so that the footprints can all go in the same direction when finished.
4. Discuss the research process with the students, placing the boot prints one by one on the floor.
5. If part of the process seems unclear to the students, add more detailed steps.
6. Boot prints can be placed on a bulletin board so class members can trace the "trail" as they work through the research unit. Or a worksheet could be made for students to record the steps they will need to follow to complete the research.
7. Remember, the number of steps required will vary for each assignment and sometimes each student.

Have an idea. (Or, teacher gives assignment.)
Determine subject.
Form questions.
Think of other key words.
Look up information.
Take notes. (This may need to be more specific:)
   Look subject up in card catalog.
   Find nonfiction books.
   Read and take notes.
   Use encyclopedia to look up subject and key words.
   Read and take notes.
   Find other resources (special reference book, person to interview, filmstrip).
   Record facts.
   (Or even more specific:)
     Use top line of call number to locate book on shelf.
     Find appropriate book for reading level and for answering questions.
Record each resource.
Organize notes.
Plan project.
Make project.
Share what you learned.
Evaluate.

Directions for tents

1. A student goes to the card catalog and looks up a subject for research, it may be ANY subject.

2. When a card is found for a nonfiction book on the subject, the top line of the call number is written on the top line of the tent flap.

3. The student then finds that number on the books in the nonfiction section of the library media center.

4. When a book is found that the student can and would like to read, the rest of the tent is filled out (author, title, and rest of call number).

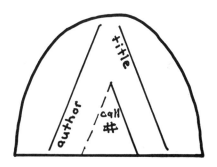

Directions for snowballs

1. The student cuts out some snowflakes and a few four inch circles.
2. On the snowflakes he records facts about the subject from the book listed on the tent.
3. One fact should be written on each snowflake; it need not be in a complete sentence.
4. The student groups together facts on the same facet of the topic (or notes that would answer the same question).
5. Snowballs can be designed to help group the snowflakes. The topic (or the question the facts answer) should be written in the center of a circle and the appropriate snowflakes glued on around outside edge.

Directions for Radio Message Worksheet

Using the facts obtained in the research, the student plans his message to send to a friend. The message should be written in his own words on the radio.

Directions for puppet or mask

A student decorates a paper bag with his face or an appropriate face for the subject. For example, if he studies space, the puppet might resemble an astronaut. The student then uses the puppet or mask either to tell how he got the information (boot prints) or what he learned about the subject (Radio Message worksheet).

Directions for pennant

The student personalizes pennant with words and pictures to describe what was learned or the joy of self in celebration of climbing Mount Everest. Attach pennant to pencil or straw, if desired.

Alternate uses

Snowballs

Place several books about a subject at a center. Have each student trace snowflakes and a four inch circle onto construction paper and cut them out. Have them write authors' names on one side of the snowflake and corresponding titles on the other. They can either alphabetize the snowflakes by author's last name or by title before gluing the snowflakes onto the circle.

List authors and titles on snowflakes. Have students alphabetize them. Remind them to omit A, An, and The when it is the FIRST word of a title. The snowflakes may be numbered on the back so the students can check their own alphabetizing.

To keep track of which notes came from which source, students can color coordinate the snowflakes and the tents: facts written in blue could represent notes from one book (decorate correct tent with blue); yellow facts and tent, another.

Tents

Write the title of the book on a tent. The student must use the card catalog to locate the author and the call number. This information is then written on the tent.

Write a subject on a tent. The student looks it up in an encyclopedia and records the title, volume, and page number.

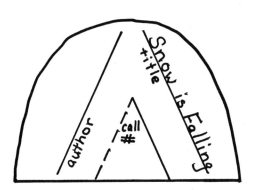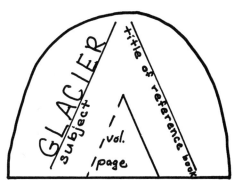

Symbolic representations

Boot prints: Path we must tread to complete research.

Tent: Home of information.

Snowflakes: Facts can flutter all around. We decide which facts we want to use and remember.

Snowball: Holds facts close together; can be used to sort out related facts.

Radio Message: Message we send to others should be in our own words.

Puppet: Research should be shared. Sometimes it is easier when we have a simple prop.

BOOT PRINT PATTERNS

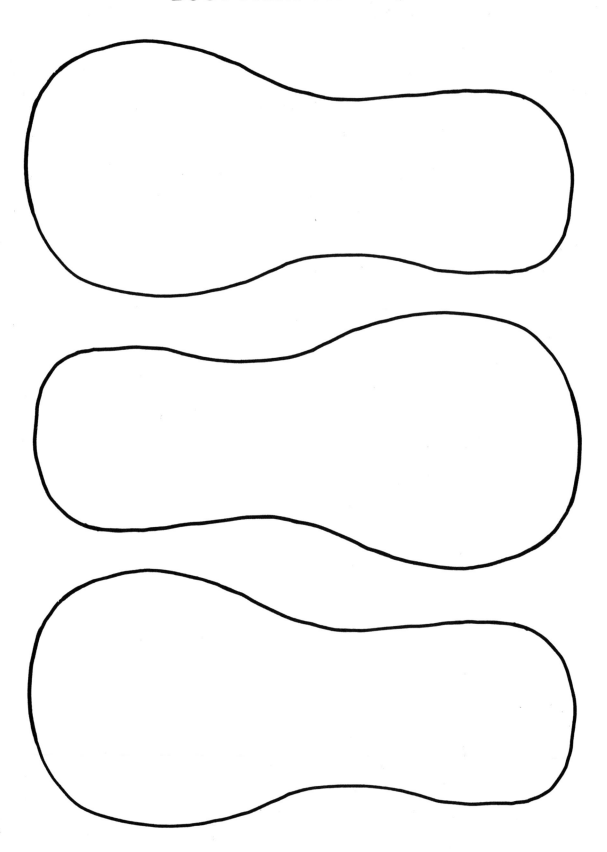

Climb Mount Everest

TENT PATTERNS

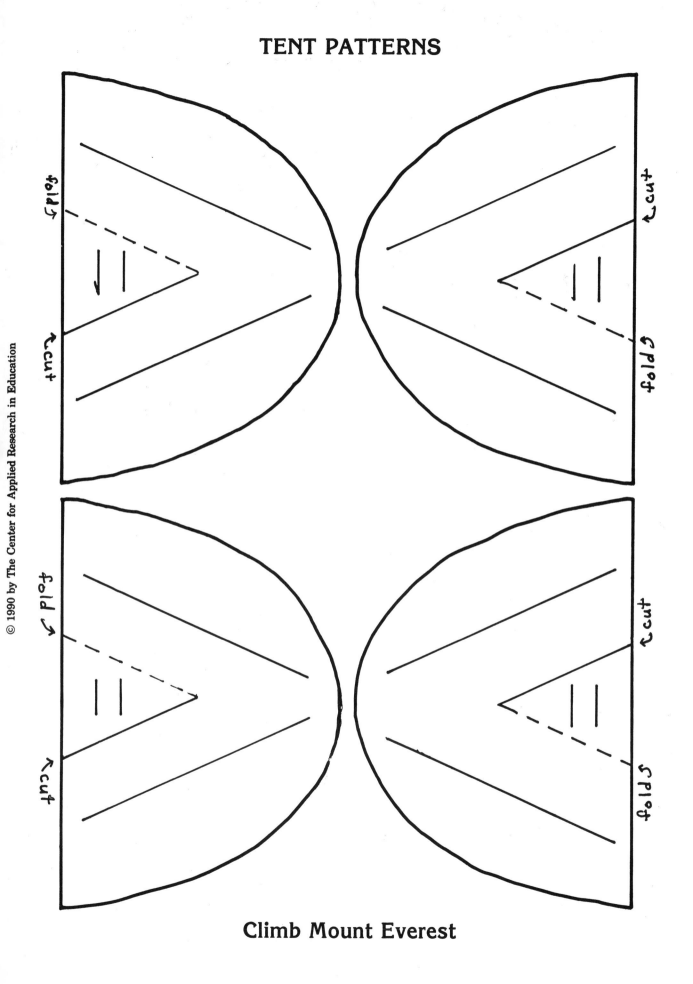

Climb Mount Everest

SNOWFLAKE PATTERN

Climb Mount Everest

Radio Message
Worksheet

Name

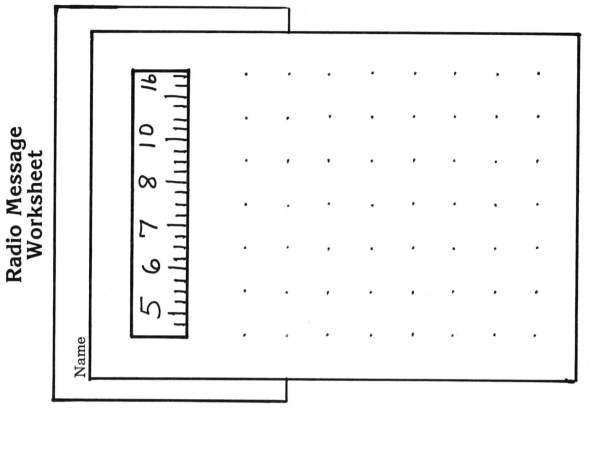

Radio Message
Worksheet

Name

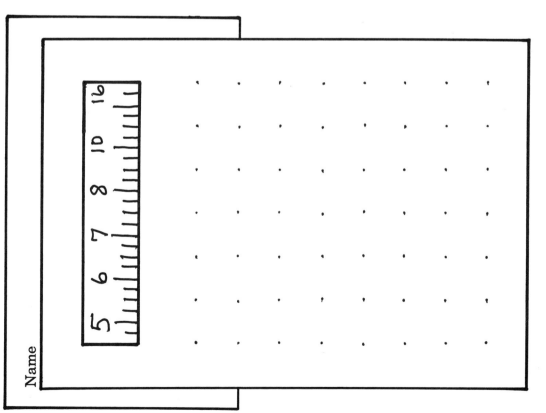

PENNANT PATTERN

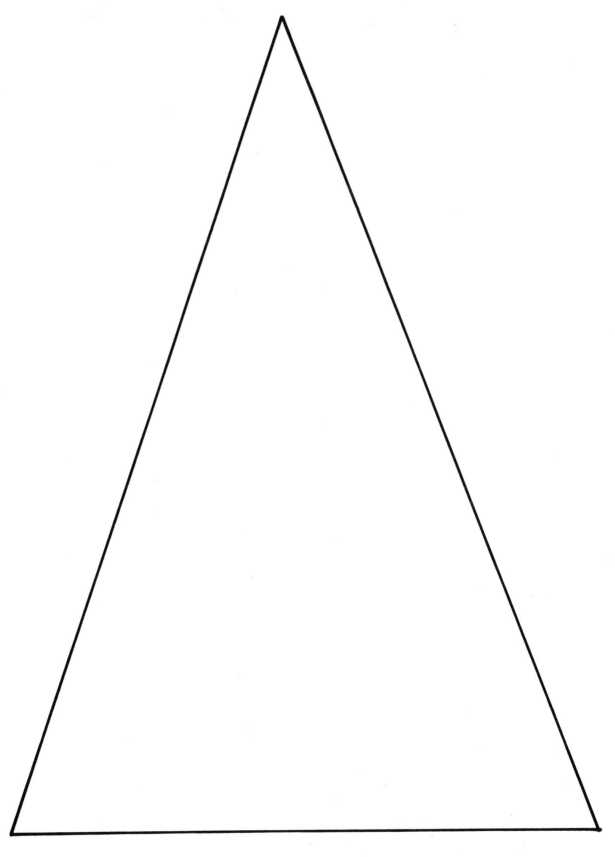

Climb Mount Everest

READING WREATHS

Skills Reinforced

Reading
Writing bibliographies

Type of Activity

Individual
Art
Paper and pencil

Grade Level: 1–6

Time Required

Two or more sessions

Prerequisite

A lesson on bibliographic information

Materials

Reading Record Cards (choose either primary or intermediate cards)
Manila envelopes, (9 × 12 inches) one for each child
Circle pattern (6 ½ inches diameter) cut from poster board or cardboard
Blank shape patterns duplicated on colored paper
Crayons or colored markers
Glue
Lined paper for each student
Pencils or pens

Procedure for Decorating Envelopes

1. Students should trace the circle pattern lightly in the center of the front of a manila envelope.

2. Each student should cut out of construction paper five or six blank shapes.

3. The shapes should be glued to the envelope using the circle line as a guide.

4. In the center of the circle each student should write his or her name, an apostrophe and an *s* ('s). Underneath the name the student should write "Reading Wreath."

5. Students may finish decorating the wreath with crayons or markers. Envelopes may be laminated, if desired.

6. Students record books as they read them on the Reading Record Cards and store the Reading Record Cards in the envelopes.

7. At the end of each grading period, semester, or other desired term, have the students alphabetize their Reading Record Cards by the author's last name. If they have read books by the same author, those cards must be alphabetized by title (skip the first word of the title if it is *The, A,* or *An*).

8. Students are to write their own bibliography on lined paper using the following formats:
   Author (last name, first name). Title. Publisher. (primary grades)
   Author (last name, first name). Title. City. Publisher, Date. (intermediate grades)

Note: Reading Record Cards can be modified so that bibliography skills are gradually developed over the years. Keep it simple in the lower grades and add something each year so that by sixth grade students are required to use the full, correct format (see chart).

Bibliographic information

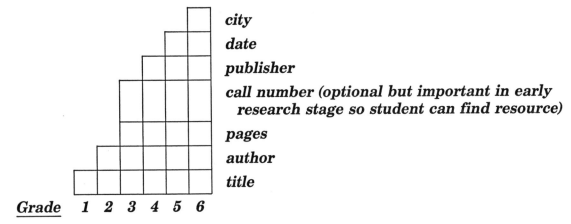

city

date

publisher

call number (optional but important in early research stage so student can find resource)

pages

author

title

Grade   *1   2   3   4   5   6*

Variations

- Have students design their own shapes for other months, seasons, and subjects (for example, snowmen, shamrocks, bunnies, eggs, and flowers). Have them cut the shapes out of construction paper.

- Create mobiles using the shapes. Have students write down an author's name on a shape and then look it up in the card catalog. Find a title by that author and write it down on the back side of the shape.

- Students can keep reading lists and suggestions from teachers and friends inside the envelope.

- Students can decorate teacher/librarian generated bibliographies to be sent home to parents. These might include: new books list, highlights of reading genre (for example, science fiction, historical fiction), award winners, seasonal reading, subject and grade level reading lists.

- Students might create an appropriate wreath to accompany a bibliography for a research project, a holiday or birthday wish list, or a bibliography of class favorites.

Follow-up Activities

FRACTURED BIBLIOGRAPHIES
RECORD THAT SOURCE

READING RECORD CARDS (PRIMARY)

author:

_____

title:

_____

publisher:

_____

author:

_____

title:

_____

publisher:

_____

author:

_____

title:

_____

publisher:

_____

author:

_____

title:

_____

publisher:

_____

author:

_____

title:

_____

publisher:

_____

author:

_____

title:

_____

publisher:

_____

READING RECORD CARDS (INTERMEDIATE)

author: _____

title: _____

city: _____

publisher: _____

copyright date: _____

number of pages: _____

Write a short summary on the back.

author: _____

title: _____

city: _____

publisher: _____

copyright date: _____

number of pages: _____

Write a short summary on the back.

author: _____

title: _____

city: _____

publisher: _____

copyright date: _____

number of pages: _____

Write a short summary on the back.

author: _____

title: _____

city: _____

publisher: _____

copyright date: _____

number of pages: _____

Write a short summary on the back.

author: _____

title: _____

city: _____

publisher: _____

copyright date: _____

number of pages: _____

Write a short summary on the back.

author: _____

title: _____

city: _____

publisher: _____

copyright date: _____

number of pages: _____

Write a short summary on the back.

FRACTURED BIBLIOGRAPHIES

Skills Reinforced

Recognizing and assembling bibliographic information in the proper order

Type of Activity

Center

Grade Level: 3+

Time Required

Two sessions

Prerequisites

READING WREATHS
Lessons on bibliographic information

Materials

File folder for center
Fractured Bibliographies cards reproduced onto card stock, laminated, and cut apart
Five letter-size envelopes
Answer keys reproduced and glued into file folder
Fractured Bibliography answer sheets reproduced in multiple copies:
Element Identification
Bibliographic Format

Preliminary Procedure

1. Sort Fractured Bibliographies cards by sets.
2. Place each set in an envelope and label the envelopes (see illustration).
3. Place the envelopes in a labeled file folder.
4. Glue the answer keys inside the file folder. Note: White out answers for the test set.
5. Have copies of the answer sheets available with the file folder in a center.

Procedure for Element Identification Answer Sheet

1. A student opens an envelope and looks at the cards to determine which ones have bibliographic information on them. Extra pieces, if any, can be placed back in the envelope.

2. The student identifies the elements on the cards and records them on an Element Identification Answer Sheet.

3. The student puts all the cards back in the envelope and picks another set to do. This continues until the student has finished all but the test set.

4. The student checks his work against the Element Identification answer key before completing the test set.

5. The teacher checks the test set answers.

6. When the student can correctly identify bibliographic information and has had a lesson on the proper written format, he is ready to use the Bibliographic Format Answer Sheet.

Procedure for Bibliographic Format Answer Sheet

1. The student pulls the cards from an envelope and places them on the table in correct bibliographic order.

2. The student records the information on the Bibliographic Format Answer Sheet using correct punctuation and spacing.

3. The student checks her work with the Bibliographic Format answer key before completing the test set.

4. The teacher checks the test set answers.

Variation

Make more Fractured Bibliographies cards and answer keys for additional resources, including magazine articles and filmstrips.

Follow-up Activity

RECORD THAT SOURCE

Answer Key

Fractured Bibliographies
Element Identification
Answer Sheet

	Author	Title	City	Publisher	Date
1.	Alvin and Virginia Silverstein	*Nature's Champions*	New York	Random House	1980
2.	Satoshi Kitamura	*Paper Jungle*	New York	Holt, Rinehart & Winston	1986
3.	Sara D. Toney	*Smithsonian Surprises*	Washington, D. C.	Smithsonian Institution Press	1985
4.	Jane Dallinger and Sylvia Johnson	*The World of Frogs and Toads*	Minneapolis	Lerner Publications	1982
5.	Mary J. Shapiro	*How They Built the Statue of Liberty*	New York	Random House	1985
Test	Carol Fenner	*Gorilla Gorilla*	New York	Random House	1973

Answer Key

Fractured Bibliographies
Bibliographic Format
Answer Sheet

1. Silverstein, Alvin and Virginia. *Nature's Champions*. New York: Random House, 1980.

2. Kitamura, Satoshi. *Paper Jungle*. New York: Holt, Rinehart & Winston, 1986.

3. Dallinger, Jane and Sylvia Johnson. *The World of Frogs and Toads*. Minneapolis: Lerner Publications Co., 1982.

4. Toney, Sara D. *Smithsonian Surprises*. Washington, D.C.: Smithsonian Institution Press, 1985.

5. Shapiro, Mary J. *How They Built the Statue of Liberty*. New York: Random House, 1985.

Test Fenner, Carol. *Gorilla Gorilla*. New York: Random House, 1973.

Name _____

Fractured Bibliographies
Element Identification
Answer Sheet

	Author	Title	City	Publisher	Date
1.					
2.					
3.					
4.					
5.					
Test					

Name _____

Fractured Bibliographies
Bibliographic Format
Answer Sheet

1. _____

2. _____

3. _____

4. _____

5. _____

Test _____

Alvin and Virginia Silverstein Fractured Bibliographies Set 1	Nature's Champions Fractured Bibliographies Set 1
illustrated by Jean Zallinger Fractured Bibliographies Set 1	Random House Fractured Bibliographies Set 1
New York Fractured Bibliographies Set 1	1980 Fractured Bibliographies Set 1
Satoshi Kitamura Fractured Bibliographies Set 2	Paper Jungle Fractured Bibliographies Set 2
Holt, Rinehart & Winston Fractured Bibliographies Set 2	New York Fractured Bibliographies Set 2
1986 Fractured Bibliographies Set 2	

Jane Dallinger and Sylvia Johnson

Fractured Bibliographies Set 3

The World of Frogs and Toads

Fractured Bibliographies Set 3

Minneapolis

Fractured Bibliographies Set 3

Lerner Publications Co.

Fractured Bibliographies Set 3

1982

Fractured Bibliographies Set 3

Sara D. Toney

Fractured Bibliographies Set 4

Smithsonian Surprises

Fractured Bibliographies Set 4

Washington, D.C.

Fractured Bibliographies Set 4

Smithsonian Institution Press

Fractured Bibliographies Set 4

1985

Fractured Bibliographies Set 4

Mary J. Shapiro	How They Built the Statue of Liberty
Fractured Bibliographies Set 5	Fractured Bibliographies Set 5
Illustrated by Huck Scarry	New York
Fractured Bibliographies Set 5	Fractured Bibliographies Set 5
Random House	1985
Fractured Bibliographies Set 5	Fractured Bibliographies Set 5
Carol Fenner	Gorilla Gorilla
Fractured Bibliographies Test Set	Fractured Bibliographies Test Set
Illustrated by Symeon Shimin	New York
Fractured Bibliographies Test Set	Fractured Bibliographies Test Set
Random House	1973
Fractured Bibliographies Test Set	Fractured Bibliographies Test Set

RECORD THAT SOURCE

Skills Reinforced

Recognizing and recording bibliographic information

Type of Activity

Center or group

Grade Level: 3+

Time Required

One session minimum

Prerequisites

READING WREATHS
FRACTURED BIBLIOGRAPHIES

Materials

Fairy Tale Bibliography samples (by type of resource and with types of resources
interfiled)
Resources all on one topic as for a unit (at least one of each):
nonfiction book
encyclopedia volume with bookmark indicating article intended
reference book with article indicated
magazine article
filmstrip, record, kit, or other AV resource
interview record (fill out a copy of figure below)
Record That Source worksheet, reproduced for each student
lined paper

Procedure

1. Place resources, bibliography samples, and worksheets
   in the center.
2. Student looks at each resource and records the
   information for each onto a Record That Source worksheet,
   where each element is identified.
3. Later, the student writes the final bibliography on
   lined paper following the desired model, either
   bibliography by type of resource or bibliography
   with types interfiled.
4. If all the resources are on the same topic, a title for the
   bibliography should be written at the top of the paper.

Variation

Divide the class into groups. Have enough materials so
each student is responsible for at least one resource.
Each person writes the bibliographic information for
one resource using the correct format on a 3-by-5-inch
card. Students check each other's work and then put the cards in alphabetical order.

Follow-up Activity

SCAVENGER HUNT

Sample Bibliography by Type of Resource

FAIRY TALE BIBLIOGRAPHY

BOOKS

Brett, Jan. *Goldilocks and the Three Bears*. New York: Dodd, Mead and Company, 1987.
Heyer, Marilee. *The Weaving of a Dream*. New York: Viking Kestrel, 1986.
Uchida, Yoshiko. *The Two Foolish Cats*. New York: Four Winds, 1978.
Wiesner, David. *The Loathsome Dragon*. New York: Putnam, 1987.
Zelinsky, Paul O. *Rumpelstiltskin*. New York: Dutton, 1986.

ENCYCLOPEDIA ARTICLES

"Andersen, Hans Christian." *World Book Encyclopedia*. 1987 (1:427).
"Folklore." *New Book of Knowledge*. 1987 (6:302–17).
"Grimm's Fairy Tales." *World Book Encyclopedia*. 1987 (8:387).

MAGAZINE ARTICLES

Hamilton, Virginia. "The People Could Fly: An American Black Folk Tale." *Cricket*, February 1988, pp. 21–26.
"That Pot That Would Not Stop Boiling." *Sesame Street*, March 1988, pp. 26–27.

AUDIO-VISUAL RESOURCES

America's Legendary Heroes (filmstrip and recording). Encyclopedia Britanica Corporation, 1980.
Mrs. Frisby and the Rats of NIMH (computer program). Sunburst, 1987.
The Story of the Gingerbread Man (book/cassette). Walt Disney, 1980.

INTERVIEWS

Roscoe, Helene. Librarian at Washington School, Mesa, Arizona. Interview. 22 April 1988.
Watts, Marie. Teacher at MacArthur School, Mesa, Arizona. Interview. 12 May 1987.

Sample Bibliography With Types Interfiled

FAIRY TALE BIBLIOGRAPHY

America's Legendary Heroes (filmstrip and recording). Encyclopedia Britanica Corporation, 1980.
"Andersen, Hans Christian." *World Book Encyclopedia*. 1987 (1:427).
Brett, Jan. *Goldilocks and the Three Bears*. New York: Dodd, Mead and Company, 1987.
"Folklore." *New Book of Knowledge*. 1987 (6:302–17).
"Grimm's Fairy Tales." *World Book Encyclopedia*. 1987 (8:387).
Hamilton, Virginia. "The People Could Fly: An American Black Folk Tale." *Cricket*, February 1988, pp. 21–26.
Heyer, Marilee. *The Weaving of a Dream*. New York: Viking Kestrel, 1986.
Mrs. Frisby and the Rats of NIMH (computer program). Sunburst, 1987.

"The Pot That Would Not Stop Boiling." *Sesame Street,* March 1988, pp. 26–7.

Roscoe, Helene. Librarian at Washington School, Mesa, Arizona. Interview. 22 April 1988.

The Story of the Gingerbread Man (book/cassette). Walt Disney, 1980.

Uchida, Yoshiko. *The Two Foolish Cats.* New York: Four Winds, 1978.

Watts, Marie. Teacher at MacArthur School, Mesa, Arizona. Interview. 12 May 1987.

Wiesner, David. *The Loathsome Dragon.* New York: Putnam, 1987.

Zelinsky, Paul O. *Rumpelstiltskin.* New York: Dutton, 1986.

RECORD THAT SOURCE!

Name _____   Room number _____

Subject _____   Other key words _____

NONFICTION BOOKS:

	call number	author	title	city	publisher	year
1.						
2.						
3.						

REFERENCE BOOKS:

	title of article	title	volume:page	year
1.				
2.				
3.				

MAGAZINE ARTICLES:

	author	title of article	magazine	date of mag.	page
1.					
2.					
3.					

AUDIO-VISUAL RESOURCES:

	title	type of resource	publisher	year
1.				
2.				
3.				

INTERVIEWS:

	name of person	position	address	topic	date
1.					
2.					
3.					

BRAINSTORMING

Skill Reinforced

Generating ideas and key words for later use

Type of Activity

Whole class, small group, partners, or individual
Paper and pencil

Grade Level: 2+

Time Required

One session minimum

Prerequisite

None

Materials

Overhead projector
Transparencies of picture worksheets and filled-in worksheet samples
Picture worksheets reproduced (one per group or student)
Transparency markers

Procedure

1. Select one of the picture worksheet transparencies and show it to the class.

2. Encourage students to generate ANY ideas they think of in relation to the subject. The instructor should write the ideas generated onto the transparency so that the students can concentrate on the ideas and not worry about spelling or speed in getting all the ideas written down.

3. Distribute copies of another picture worksheet to each group of four or five students.

4. Encourage students to generate ideas that are inspired by looking at the picture. One student should be the recorder. Allow five to ten minutes.

5. Read each group's list aloud. Ask if anyone else can think of a subject that could be added to the list.

6. Students may record ideas from other groups, if desired.

7. With so many ideas to choose from, students should now be able to determine which area they would like to study. Let them circle any key words on their worksheets that would be useful in finding information on their topic.

8. Inform students that they will not have to research the topic they choose. Help students realize that while at first they may not have liked the subject presented, they probably will have more enthusiasm for picking out an interesting topic after using this procedure.

9. Repeat the procedure with other pictures or write a subject in the middle of a blank transparency and proceed from that.

Note: The best approach is to group ideas as they are given. At first the teacher will have to guide the class as a whole by drawing pie shapes for primary students or network lines for older ones. (See filled-in worksheet samples.)

Variations

- Give each student the same picture worksheet. Let students record ideas within a specified time limit. Group students and have them share ideas. Share group lists with the class. Or, see which student comes up with the most ideas in the time specified.

- Record all the ideas generated by the class on one worksheet and place it somewhere in the room so all students can look at it and add any other ideas to it when they think of any.

- Have students generate questions about a topic. When the list is long enough, let students pick the best three and look up the answers.

- Have students make an outline using the ideas written on their brainstorming worksheet.

- Make additional brainstorming worksheets using illustrations from clip art books, bulletin board idea books, newspapers, and other sources.

- An excellent topic for class discussion is reference resources. Have students as a class make a composite list of all kinds of resources available for information. Encourage students to refer to the list and to use a variety of resources as they research. In fact, the contents could be turned into an individual checklist for indicating types of resources used in a project.

Follow-up Activity
THE UMBRELLA EFFECT

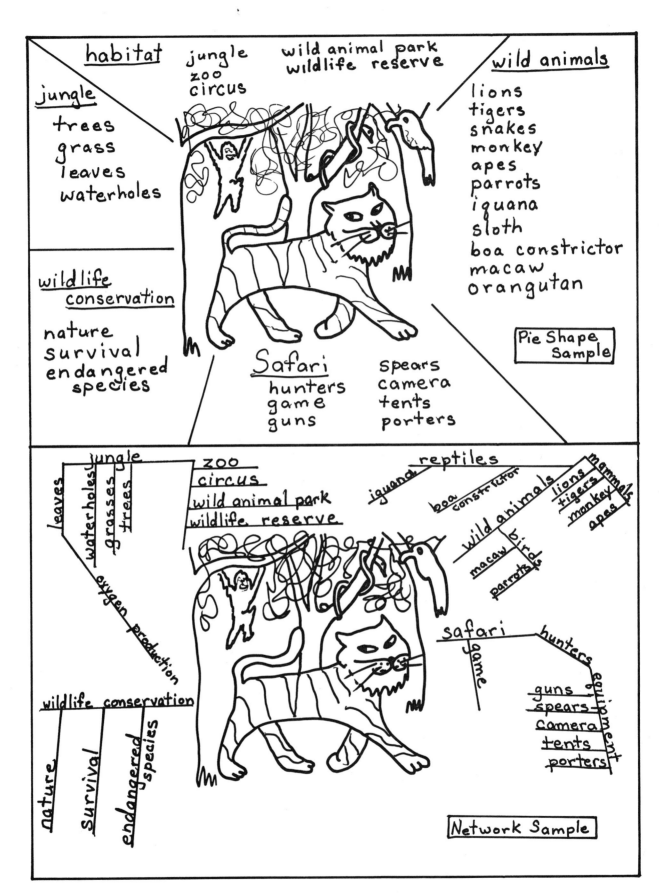

habitat   jungle   wild animal park   wild animals
           zoo   wildlife reserve
           circus

jungle   lions
  trees   tigers
  grass   snakes
  leaves   monkey
  waterholes   apes
                                          parrots
                                          iguana
                                          sloth
                                          boa constrictor
wildlife   macaw
  conservation   orangutan

  nature   Pie Shape
  survival   Sample
  endangered
    species   Safari   spears
                      hunters   camera
                      game   tents
                      guns   porters

jungle   zoo   reptiles
leaves   circus
waterholes   wild animal park   iguana   boa   wild animals   lions   mammals
grasses   wildlife reserve   constrictor   tigers
trees   monkey
                                                        macaw   bird   apes
         oxygen production   parrots

                                              safari   hunters
                                                game   equipment
wildlife conservation   guns
                                                                spears
nature survival endangered species   camera
                                                                tents
                                                                porters

                                              Network Sample

Name(s) _____

BRAINSTORMING WORKSHEET A

BRAINSTORMING WORKSHEET B

Name(s) _____

BRAINSTORMING WORKSHEET C

Name(s) ——————

BRAINSTORMING WORKSHEET D

Name(s) ——————

BRAINSTORMING WORKSHEET E

THE UMBRELLA EFFECT

Skill Reinforced

Determining key words relating to research subject

Type of Activity

Whole class, small group, partners, or individual
Paper and pencil

Grade Level: 3–6

Time Required

One session minimum

Prerequisite

BRAINSTORMING
Lesson on key words and subject headings

Materials

Overhead projector
Transparency of The Umbrella Effect Worksheet samples, if desired
Transparency of The Umbrella Effect Worksheet
The Umbrella Effect Worksheet reproduced in multiple copies
Sears List of Subject Headings, edited by Barbara Wetby. H. W. Wilson.
Transparency markers

Procedure

1. Show the transparency of the worksheet to the class.
2. Select a subject the class is studying, for example, insects or Benjamin Franklin, and fill out the transparency worksheet as a group.
3. Repeat this several times throughout the year with various subjects.
4. When the class as a whole becomes adept at coming up with appropriate key words, divide the class into groups and let them generate key words for a class research subject. Key words from all groups can be compiled for class use.
5. Individuals can and should use the worksheet for independent research projects. However, until they are adept at generating key words by themselves, it is best (and less frustrating) if they are allowed input from classmates.

Note: This worksheet is mainly a guide to encourage students to think of alternatives before they get to the resources and find they have to use other key words to find their chosen subject. Consequently, it will not fit each subject exactly. Sometimes the umbrella will have too many sections, other times not enough. Sometimes not all the raindrops will need to be used; other times more should be added. Samples are included for instructor/class perusal. Encourage older students to look at Sears List of Subject Headings *for ideas.*

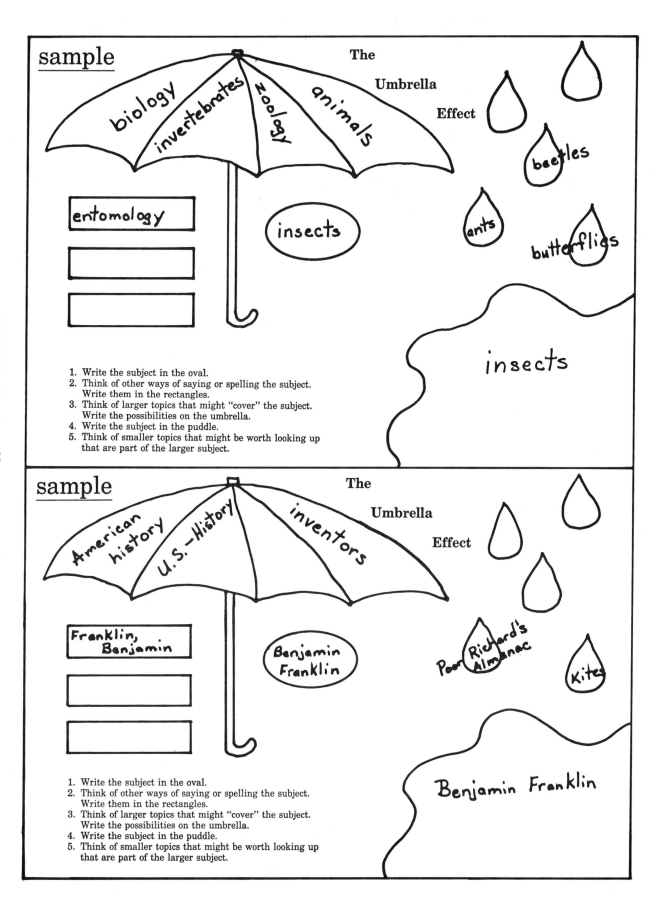

sample

biology invertebrates zoology animals

The Umbrella Effect

entomology

insects

beetles

ants

butterflies

insects

1. Write the subject in the oval.
2. Think of other ways of saying or spelling the subject. Write them in the rectangles.
3. Think of larger topics that might "cover" the subject. Write the possibilities on the umbrella.
4. Write the subject in the puddle.
5. Think of smaller topics that might be worth looking up that are part of the larger subject.

sample

American history U.S.–History inventors

The Umbrella Effect

Franklin, Benjamin

Benjamin Franklin

Poor Richard's Almanac

Kites

Benjamin Franklin

1. Write the subject in the oval.
2. Think of other ways of saying or spelling the subject. Write them in the rectangles.
3. Think of larger topics that might "cover" the subject. Write the possibilities on the umbrella.
4. Write the subject in the puddle.
5. Think of smaller topics that might be worth looking up that are part of the larger subject.

Name _____

The
Umbrella
Effect

1. Write the subject in the oval.
2. Think of other ways of saying or spelling the subject.
   Write them in the rectangles.
3. Think of larger topics that might "cover" the subject.
   Write the possibilities on the umbrella.
4. Write the subject in the puddle.
5. Think of smaller topics that might be worth looking up
   that are part of the larger subject.

SCAVENGER HUNT

Skill Reinforced

Finding a variety of resources on a particular subject

Type of Activity

Whole class game

Grade Level: 4+

Time Required

One session minimum

Prerequisites

BRAINSTORMING
THE UMBRELLA EFFECT
RECORD THAT SOURCE

Materials

Record That Source worksheet (see RECORD THAT SOURCE)

Procedure

1. Select a general topic for class research.
2. Brainstorm and identify key words as a class, if desired.
3. Assign students into pairs and let them find as many resources in the library media center as they can on the class topic.
4. When a resource is located, one of the pair stays and keeps track of where the book or resource belongs while the other student shows the library media specialist or teacher what they have found (chapter, pages, or whole resource).
5. If the material is appropriate, it is placed on a book cart or stacked on a table. Inappropriate resources are placed back where they belong. That is why one student stays where the resource was found.
6. Each pair continues to find additional resources in the time allowed.

Note: This is best used when first introducing a new unit or project, for example, insects, space, Civil War. Students will have assembled resources and will be aware of what is available to start research. A more refined search for materials can be conducted if specific information is still lacking.

Variations

- Instead of placing materials on a chart or table, have students record resources on cards or on a Record That Source worksheet.
- The class can be divided into three or four teams. Points may be given for the number of resources found; points may be deducted for inappropriate resources.
- If an entire grade level is researching the same general topic, points could be given to the class that does the best sleuthing and finds the most resources. All resources will have to be put back on the shelves by each pair of students except during the last class. A written bibliography is a must. The librarian, teacher, or a student could then locate all resources found by all the classes. With the materials on a cart, each class can have time with all the available materials, and individual students will have better access.

Follow-up Activity

Actual research or classroom activities using the materials collected.

THAT'S A FACT!

Skills Reinforced
Recognizing and organizing facts

Type of Activity
Whole class art

Grade Level: K–3

Time Required
Three or more sessions

Prerequisite
Know the difference between fact and fiction

Materials
Easy nonfiction books on subjects of interest (animal books are excellent, as are the "New True Books" from Children's Press, which are written at the second grade level)
Index cards (3 by 5 inches)
Drawing paper
Crayons

Procedure

1. Read a nonfiction book aloud to the class. Each time the students hear a fact they think they should remember, they raise their hands.
2. The teacher records each fact on a 3-by-5-inch card in note form (not as a sentence) using the student's wording, not the book's.
3. When there are more facts than students, let each student choose one fact and illustrate it. Be sure to record the student's name on the fact card.
4. Have students write their fact as a sentence on the note card.
5. Have students copy their sentence directly onto the art page or onto a separate piece of paper that can be glued on later.
6. Show the students the completed pages and ask the children how the facts can be grouped (for example, what the animal looks like, what it eats, where it lives).

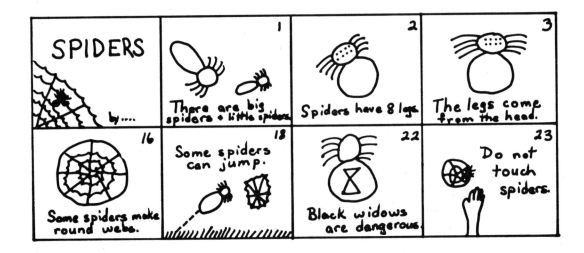

218

7. Distribute pages back to students. Then name a fact group and ask students to hand in their page if it belongs to that group.

8. Continue until all papers are collected.

9. Encourage students to help organize the pages within each group.

10. Number the pages, mount on construction paper if desired, and laminate the pages. Punch holes on one side and bind with yarn.

11. Display the class books for students and parents to enjoy.

Follow-up Activity

LET YOUR KNOWLEDGE BLOSSOM!

MONSTER NOTEBOOK

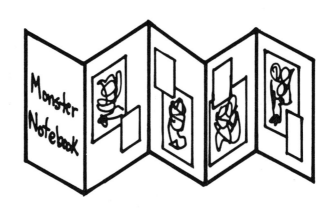

Skill Reinforced

Notetaking

Type of Activity

Whole class art

Grade Level: 3+

Time Required

Two sessions

Prerequisite

THAT'S A FACT!

Materials

Monster Notebook worksheet reproduced for each student
Crayons
Pencils

Procedure

1. Distribute Monster Notebook worksheets to students.

2. Have students draw pictures of monsters in the "Draw a monster" box. Be sure to talk over suggestions for making pictures "monstery."

3. Assign each student a different number and have him record the number in the two boxes marked with a #. (When page is cut apart later this will be needed for proper identification.)

4. Collect the papers and shuffle them.

5. Distribute the pictures so notes can be taken by another student; student should *not* have his own picture.

6. Discuss notetaking with the students. It should not be a list such as "tomato, lettuce, cheese on a hot sesame seed bun." Write a sample list such as this one on the chalkboard:

   3 eyes
   purple face
   green spots on legs
   tiny trickle of blood from arm
   spines down back
   nose on right ear

7. Have students take notes on the picture they have in the "Take notes on the monster" space.

8. Have students star the one most important note—the one that really describes the picture.

9. Collect the papers.

10. Cut the papers in half.

11. A week later, lay the pictures out on the floor or pin them to a bulletin board.

12. Read the starred note for one picture and have the students identify that picture from all the rest. It may be necessary to read all the notes for that picture.

13. If the number on the picture and the notes match, place the two halves together out of the way.
14. Sometimes the picture cannot be identified even with all the notes; put that notesheet towards the bottom of the pile and read it later when there are fewer pictures from which to choose.
15. Talk to the students about what they have learned about notetaking. The discussion should include the following points:

    There is no set number of notes to take. Sometimes one fact is enough; other times you need a lot of facts.
    Notetaking is fun.

Follow-up Activities

Mount the pictures and the matching notes on construction paper. Tape the sheets together into an accordian book for students to look at. Parents or students could type notes for easier legibility.

Have the students write a description of a monster using only the notes.

Draw a monster! Sign as artist.

Monster Notebook Worksheet

Artist:

Notetaker:

Take notes on the monster! Sign as notetaker.

LET YOUR KNOWLEDGE BLOSSOM!

Skills Reinforced

Recognizing and organizing facts

Type of Activity

Whole class, small group, partners, or individual
Paper and pencil

Grade Level: 2+

Time Required

One session; new copies of worksheets can be used many times for various research projects

Prerequisite

THAT'S A FACT!

Materials

Transparency of Let Your Knowledge Blossom worksheet
Let Your Knowledge Blossom worksheet reproduced in multiple copies
Additional worksheets, if desired:
  Nest Full of Notes
  Travel to the Stars
  Field of Daisies
  The Clipboards
Transparency markers
Easy nonfiction books on subjects of interest ("New True Books" from Children's Press are excellent, as they are written at the second grade level and have an index.)

Procedure

1. Pick a topic of interest to most students, for example, whales.

2. Show the students a nonfiction book on the subject. Use it to fill out the center of the flower on the transparency.

3. Read the book aloud and have students raise their hands when they hear a fact they want to remember.

4. Fill in the daisy petal by petal, recording only one fact in each. Wording of the students is to be used, not the wording of the book. Recorded facts may be single words, *short* phrases, or simple diagrams; they are *not* to be in complete sentences.

5. Distribute copies of the Let Your Knowledge Blossom worksheet. Let students work as partners or independently to prepare individual flowers.

6. Students pick a topic of interest and find an appropriate book on the subject.

7. Have them fill in the center of their flower with the information requested. Then have them enter facts they locate using their notetaking skills.

8. If students are interested in continuing their research, let them have additional worksheets and encourage them to look in different resources.

Note: Encourage the use of the thesaurus! If a student feels she must copy a word from the resource, let her copy it but put a box around the word. Have her use the thesaurus to find another word. She then writes the new word next to the boxed word and crosses out the box (Sample A). When using the facts for a written or oral report, she should use the new word or think of an even better word.

Variations

- Use additional worksheets:

  Nest Full of Notes

  Travel to the Stars

  Treemendous Notes (see FROM WHICH TREE DID I FALL?)

- The notetaking forms were designed for nonfiction books. It is easy to adjust them for recording bibliographic information from a reference book:

author	changes to	subject or entry word
title	stays	title
call number	changes to	volume number
page(s)	stays	page(s)

Follow-up Activity

When students are adept at recording individual facts, show them how to organize their information so like facts are grouped together (see Sample B). This allows them to record more facts and facilitates the use of the index of a nonfiction book to locate appropriate information. It also gives students a head start when it comes to writing or orally giving a report. Students are now ready to use Field of Daisies or The Clipboards for worksheets. Let Your Knowledge Blossom, Nest full of Notes, and Travel to the Stars can also be used as long as students underline or somehow identify the type of information in each petal, egg, or star.

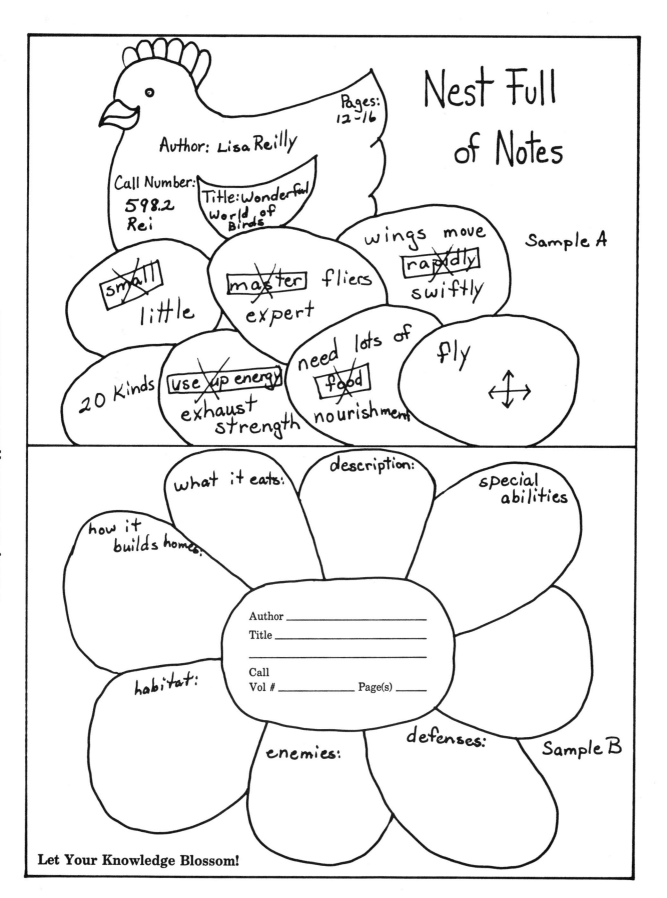

Nest Full of Notes

Pages: 12-16

Author: Lisa Reilly

Call Number: 598.2 Rei

Title: Wonderful World of Birds

Sample A

small — little

master — expert fliers

wings move rapidly — swiftly

20 kinds

use up energy — exhaust strength

need lots of food — nourishment

fly

what it eats:

description:

special abilities

how it builds homes:

Author _____
Title _____
_____
Call
Vol # _____ Page(s) _____

habitat:

enemies:

defenses:

Sample B

Let Your Knowledge Blossom!

Name _____

fact:

fact:

fact:

fact:

Author _____
Title _____
_____
Call _____
Vol # _____ Page(s) _____

fact:

fact:

fact:

fact:

Let your knowledge blossom!

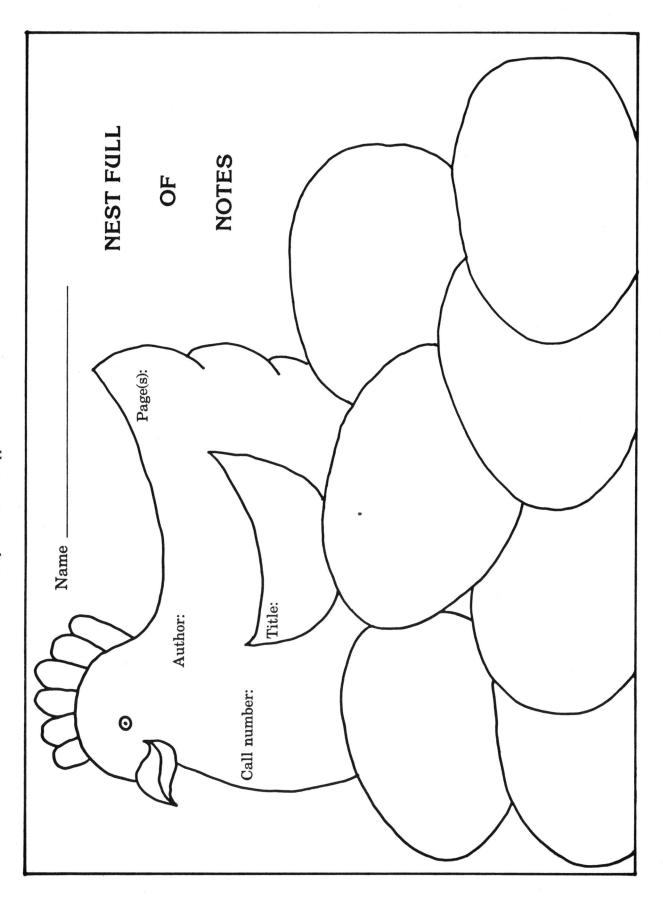

NEST FULL

OF

NOTES

Name _____

Page(s):

Author:

Title:

Call number:

Name _____

Travel to the Stars

Call number:

Author:

Title:

Page(s):

Name _____

FIELD OF DAISIES

Author:

Title:

Call number:

Page(s):

topic:

fact:

fact:

Name _____

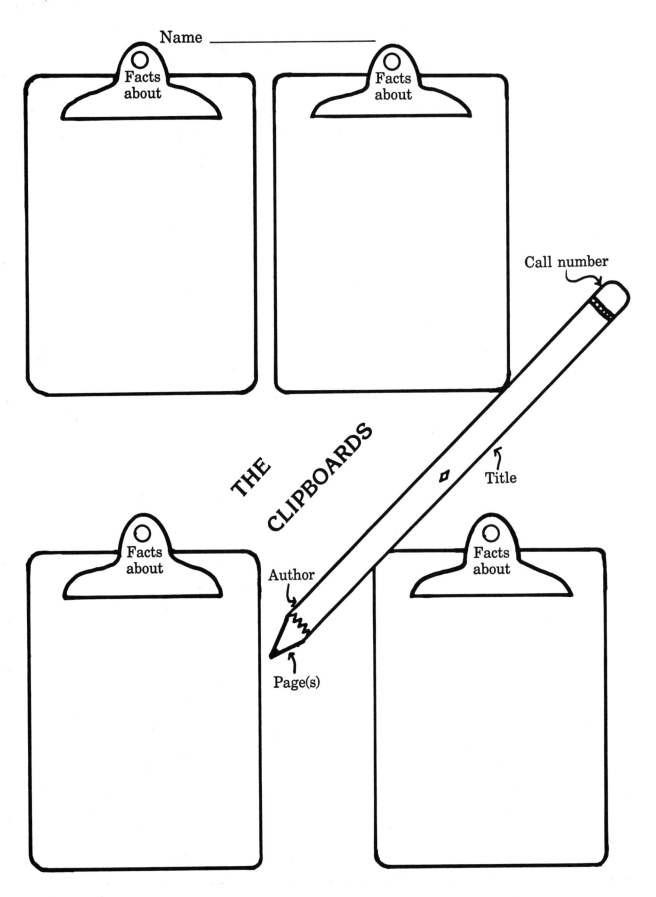

Facts about

Facts about

Call number

THE
CLIPBOARDS

Title

Facts about

Author

Facts about

Page(s)

RESEARCH IMAGERY

Skill Reinforced

Visualizing the research process

Type of Activity

Whole class movement

Grade Level: 2–6

Time Required

At least one session, but procedure can be used many times in various research projects

Prerequisites

LE GRAND TOUR
CARD CATALOG SEARCH (may be concurrent)
ENCYCLOPEDIA SEARCH (may be concurrent)
CLIMB MOUNT EVEREST (may be concurrent)
LET YOUR KNOWLEDGE BLOSSOM (may be concurrent)
Introduction to using basic research tools (card catalog, encyclopedias)

Procedure

1. Determine the research project students are to do.

2. Walk through the research process, showing the students the materials they will use and places they will have to go to, that is, show an encyclopedia set including the index volume, walk over to the card catalog and pull out a drawer for a specific topic, and find a book on the reference shelf.

3. Explain and show the students what they will probably need to do for their research project.

4. Then have them close their eyes and review what was just shown to them in story form (see sample stories below). Students should imagine themselves walking through the project.

5. Make up new stories to fit each research project. Be sure to explain and show any new steps to students before they are to imagine themselves doing it.

Note: Research Imagery can be used before the students start their research, while they are doing their research, or after they are done. It can help them visualize today's step in the research process or give them ideas to try next time. Be sure to include a variety of resources in the stories and any areas where students are likely to have or have been having problems. Seeing themselves in their minds step by step solving the problems helps them when they actually are facing the situation.

Sample Story for Primary Grades

You have picked whales for your subject. Today you need to look up information in an encyclopedia. You walk into the media center and turn to the right, because you know that the reference area is right around the checkout desk. You pick the *W* volume of an encyclopedia. Using the guide words, you locate an article entitled "Whales and Other Sea Mammals." You write down five facts you want to remember and start to close the book. Wait! You almost forgot to write down the page number. After writing down the title of the encyclopedia, the article title, and volume and page numbers, you look at the list of related articles at the end and pick some words to write in your key word bank. Next time you can look up one of these. You put the volume back where it belongs, push your chair under the table, and go back to class. You are happy with what you have done today.

Sample Story for Intermediate Grades

Your teacher has just given you an assignment in your science class. You are to write a report on insects. You know that *insects* is a big subject and you really aren't too interested in bugs anyway. What are you going to do?

Well, you think about the different kinds of bugs you know about: flies, bees, ladybugs. . . you know there's got to be more. So you sit down and decide to write down all the things you know about insects to see if that will give you any ideas about what you would like to research. Then you go to the library to look up some information about insects in general to see what kind of information you'll be able to find on the subjects that appeal to you. In looking in the card catalog and the encyclopedias you find there is lots of information and you are going to have to narrow the subject down even more. You finally decide to look at how insects use their senses of sight, hearing, taste, touch, and smell.

You visit a natural history museum and see that there are more bugs than you thought possible. You call a pest store to see which senses they try to appeal to in killing bugs. You have been writing down bits of information that have been interesting to you on little slips of paper or 3-by-5-inch cards. You have also collected a pamphlet from the museum and the pest control company sent you some information. You find an article in *Ranger Rick Magazine* and decide to pursue this further by looking in the *National Geographic Index* where you see a number of articles listed. You keep adding to your list of where you are finding interesting bits of information.

It's time to start thinking about your project. You talk to the library media specialist, and she shows you some pictures of projects that other students have done on other subjects. There are a lot to choose from: dioramas, charts, bulletin boards, skits, and puppets. You decide that you want to make a great big circle on poster board and divide it into five sections. Each section will have the label of one of the senses and pictures of insects with notes on how that insect uses that sense. You draw out a rough draft so that you will remember what you want to do.

You make a list of all the materials you need. You go back to the library to draw the pictures that you need from the identification books. Writing neatly, you make your project. When you take it to school, everyone is pleased with your project; you know you have done your best.

Variations

- Shorten the story, focusing on the day's research step or concentrating on any problem areas in the students' research.
- Add items you have done with students (visit public library, for example).
- Use MEDIA MAZE and have students follow along while you tell the story.

Follow-up Activity

Students do research or look forward to their next successful research project.

THE RIGHT WAY!

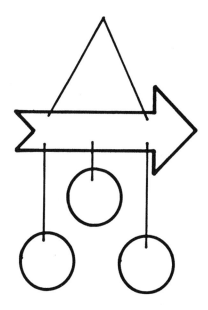

Skill Reinforced

Research skills

Type of Activity

Whole class, small group, partners, or individual
Art

Grade Level: 3–4

Time Required

One or two sessions

Prerequisites

THE UMBRELLA EFFECT
READING WREATHS or RECORD THAT SOURCE
RESEARCH IMAGERY

Materials

The Right Way mobile shapes reproduced onto card stock
Scissors
Paper punch
String or yarn
Reference sources

Procedure

1. The student cuts out the mobile shapes and thinks of a question he would like answered. The question is written on the back of the arrow.

2. The student, by himself or with other students helping, determines the key words he would use to look up the answer to the question in the card catalog or index to a reference book. These words are written on the back of the "Key Word" circle.

3. When the answer is located, it is written in note or sentence form (in the student's own words) on the back of the "Answer" circle.

4. The source where the answer was found is listed on the "Source" circle.

5. The three circles near the bottom edge of the arrow and the two circles near the top edge (see diagram) should be punched. A hole is also punched near the top of each of the circles.

6. Students should attach the circles to the arrow with either string or yarn (see the illustration above). Attach a string through the top holes to hang the mobile from the ceiling.

Variation

Let students draw an outline shape of their subject on construction paper. The shape is cut out and the question is written on the back. Simple geometric or subject related shapes are drawn and cut out for the key words, answer, and source information. For example, if the question is about squirrels, a squirrel shape could be drawn and cut out. Acorn shapes could be designed for recording the additional information.

Related Activities

ANIMAL SAFARI
CLIMB MOUNT EVEREST

233

THE RIGHT WAY!
MOBILE

Directions: Cut out the shapes. Write your name on the front of each piece. Think of a question you would like answered and write it on the back of the arrow. Think of the key words you could use to help look up the needed information. Write these on the key word circle and use them to locate your information. Record the answer on the back of the answer circle. Record the source of your information on the back of the source circle.

   Punch out the circles on the pieces and attach each circle with string so they hang freely. Attach a piece of string through the two top holes. Check with your teacher before hanging up your mobile.

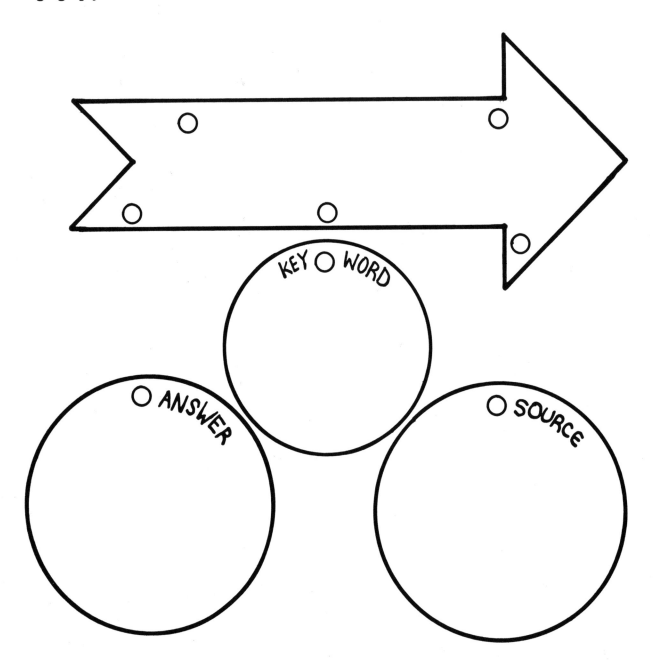

ANIMAL SAFARI

Skill Reinforced
Research skills

Type of Activity
Whole class game

Grade Level: 3+

Time Required
Two or three sessions

Prerequisites
LET YOUR KNOWLEDGE BLOSSOM!
RESEARCH IMAGERY
PUT HUMPTY DUMPTY TOGETHER AGAIN EGGS-ACTLY

Materials
Animal Safari worksheet reproduced in quantity
Animal Safari clue gameboard, reproduced onto colored card stock and laminated
Blank 2-by-2-inch cards cut from card stock (These will be referred to as Animal Safari clue cards)
Animal Safari answer sheets reproduced and cut apart
Box with a slit for inserting answers
Prizes for winners

Procedure
1. Students research the animal of their choice using the Animal Safari worksheet.
2. Wait at least one month after research is complete before starting the weekly clue game.
3. The teacher picks the set of clues to be used for the week.
4. Each clue is written on a clue card; the day of the week that the clue is to be used should be written on the back.
5. If several weeks' clues are written at one time, number each set to keep track of them.
6. Each day a clue is put up and the students are to look in the reference books to figure out what animal it is.
7. Students should be allowed one opportunity each day to put an answer on an Animal Safari Answer Sheet and put it in the box.
8. On Monday the first five students to correctly identify the animal the week before should receive a prize, perhaps an animal sticker. Only correctly spelled animal names should be accepted.

Variation
If this activity was completed in a classroom, it would be fun and appropriate to place the gameboard in the media center so students in the same grade level or in the school can research the animal from your students' clues. Fifteen winners is an appropriate number for an all-school contest. Involvement increases when weekly winners are announced over the PA system.

Hint for Library Media Specialist
Unload the answer box twice a day to curtail students entering "sneaky" dates and times on the answer sheets.

_____'s Animal Safari Worksheet

Instructions:

1. Pick the animal you want to research.
2. Think of additional words that will help you look up the subject. For example, if your subject is *whales*, other key words might include *mammal, oceanography,* and *marine animals.* Write your words on the key word line.
3. As you look up information, be sure to record where you found it in the bibliography section.
4. Write your notes in the boxes. Remember, only one note per box and do not write in complete sentences—just give the idea.
5. Let your teacher/library media specialist see your sheet and give you some suggestions for improving your research.
6. Look over your notes and pick the best. Some notes can be put together now to form one clue. Cross out boxes not to be used.
7. Decide the order clues will be given. Hard clues come first. You don't want to give your animal away the first day! Number the boxes 1 through 5 for Monday through Friday.
8. Write your clues from your notes, but this time use complete sentences.

animal: _____

key words: _____

Bibliography:

Title: _____

Author: _____ or subject: _____

Call #: _____ or volume #: _____

Page: _____

Title: _____

Author: _____ or subject: _____

Call #: _____ or volume #: _____

Page: _____

Clues:

Monday: _____

Tuesday: _____

Wednesday: _____

Thursday: _____

Friday: _____

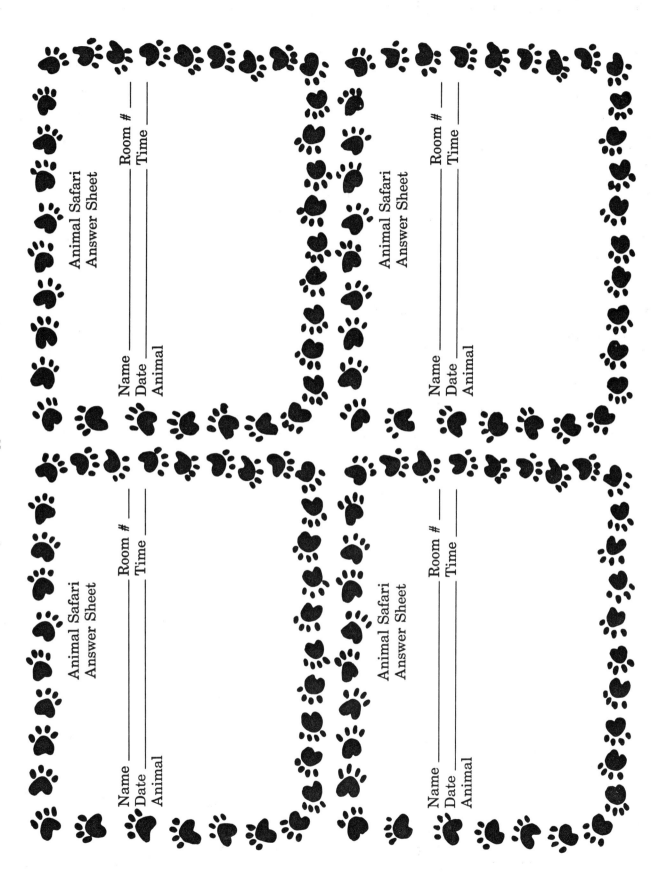

Animal Safari
Answer Sheet

Room # ——————
Time ——————

Name ——————
Date ——————
Animal ——————

Animal Safari
Answer Sheet

Room # ——————
Time ——————

Name ——————
Date ——————
Animal ——————

Animal Safari
Answer Sheet

Room # ——————
Time ——————

Name ——————
Date ——————
Animal ——————

Animal Safari
Answer Sheet

Room # ——————
Time ——————

Name ——————
Date ——————
Animal ——————

Animal Safari

Monday	Tuesday	Wednesday	Thursday	Friday

What animal are we tracking this week?

PROJECT PLANS

Skills Reinforced

organizing and planning a project

Type of Activity

individual; paper and pencil

Grade Levels: 3+

Time Required

1 session

Prerequisites

BRAINSTORMING
THE UMBRELLA EFFECT

Materials

Reproduce appropriate worksheet in multiple copies:
Project Plan A is for younger children
Project Plan B is for older students
Project Plan C is more suitable for book or poetry projects rtaher than research

Procedure

1. Students start researching topic.
2. When they have most of the research done and are ready to start putting it together, give students worksheets to plan their project.
3. Using their completed worksheet, students can finish their research and make their project.

Explanations of Each Area on Worksheet:

Subject to study	This is the topic the student is working on. It can be in key word or question format.
Key word bank	The student records additional key words relating to the subject.
What do I want to learn about my subject?	Students understand research as answering questions. So if they record what it is that they are trying to answer, they can look it up better. Older students can record the topics for which they need to find information.
What resources can I use?	Students need to be encouraged to use a variety of resources instead of just books or encyclopedias. This helps them explore other possibilities. Perhaps a resource type might be required, such as an interview or film.
What project will I make?	Research does not always need to end up as a written research paper. Sometimes a different kind of product, such as a chart or diorama, will show off the facts more effectively. Students should draw a rough draft of what their project will look like on the back of the paper. Of course, they will probably have to wait until they have done some research before they can finish this part.

What materials do I need?	Students don't always plan ahead or think of all it takes to put something together. By recording all the materials needed, students will be encouraged to have them all on hand when they start working on the project.
What steps do I follow to complete my project?	This is another effort to encourage the students to think ahead. They won't be as apt to throw the project together at the last minute.
Time it takes	Students are not expert at estimating how much time it takes to do things. If they record their estimates and compare them to the actual time they took, they can judge better for another project. With guidance they may learn not to waste time.
Date due	This lets the student know when everything is to be turned in. This part of the plan could easily be changed to fit the situation. Perhaps different sections will be due at separate times. For instance, notes might be due one week, rough drafts the next, all before the final project is due.

Variation

If students are working in a group, they should record who is to do what and when it is due.

Follow-up Activity

PROJECT AND PROJECT PLAN EVALUATION

Note. Expose students to a variety of project types i.e. charts, graphs, dioramas. Later, when students have a choice, they can be more creative.

PROJECT PLAN A

Name _____ Room number _____

Subject to study _____

Key word bank

_____ _____ _____

_____ _____ _____

_____ _____ _____

What do I want to learn about my subject?

_____

_____

_____

_____

What resources can I use?

book   encyclopedia   phone

film   interview   visit store/museum

magazine   Other _____

What project will I make? _____
   (see project list)

What materials do I need?

_____ _____ _____

_____ _____ _____

What steps do I follow to complete my project?

6.

5.

4.

3.

2.

1.

time it takes

Date due

A rough draft picture of my project is on the back.

PROJECT PLAN B

Name _____ Room number _____

Subject _____

Key word bank _____

_____

Research questions

_____

_____

_____

_____

Types of resources

_____ books   _____ interview a person

_____ encyclopedias   _____ visit a store or museum

_____ magazines   _____ other _____

Type of project _____

Materials needed to produce project

_____

_____

_____

Steps to make project

_____

_____

_____

_____

Estimated timetable   Actual timetable

   plan _____ days/weeks   plan _____ days/weeks

   research _____ days/weeks   research _____ days/weeks

   project _____ days/weeks   project _____ days/weeks

Date due _____

PROJECT PLAN C

Name _____

Type of project _____

Date project is due: _____

Materials needed to produce project:

_____

_____

_____

Steps to make project:

1. _____

2. _____

3. _____

4. _____

5. _____

Draw rough draft of project:

PROJECT PLAN C

Name _____

Type of project _____

Date project is due: _____

Materials needed to produce project:

_____

_____

_____

Steps to make project:

1. _____

2. _____

3. _____

4. _____

5. _____

Draw rough draft of project:

PROJECT FILE

Skill Reinforced

Using a variety of projects

Type of Activity

Art

Grade Level: All

Time Required

Varies; depends on project and number of activities used

Prerequisite

PROJECT PLANS (see Project Plan C)—concurrent

Materials

Project List
Three-ring notebook or photo album
Camera
Film
Other materials vary, as appropriate for project selected

Procedure

1. The teacher selects a project type from the Project List for all students to use (for example, for a book report). Perhaps the students are to write an advertisement to sell their favorite book or dress up as a character in the book. (Each time a book report is due, a different project type is required.)

2. Take photographs of the projects done by the students in your (or other) class(es). For example, take a picture of a student being a radio announcer.

3. Attach the picture (along with a copy of the script in this example) on a page in the notebook.

4. Label the picture as to the type of project (in this case a radio broadcast).

5. Organize the notebook so that all the pictures of student–made bulletin boards, or greeting cards, or maps, etc., are grouped together so students can see the variety of ideas even for one project type.

6. Let students browse through the notebook when it is time for them to plan a new project. Not only do they enjoy looking at pictures of fellow classmates, but it gives them the incentive to say, "I can do it too!"

Variation

Use the Project List as a checklist. Students check off the types of projects they have done. They are then encouraged to try something new.

Follow-up Activity

PROJECT AND PROJECT PLAN EVALUATIONS

Notes

A new notebook doesn't have to be started each year. Just add pages (or leave pages blank to fill in in later years). The variety gets better and better. Through the years, pictures of many kinds of projects will be illustrated.

Once students have already done a project, such as a diorama, they will find it easier to choose it as a project type for future research projects. Consequently, if teachers in each grade level throughout the school coordinate their plans for a variety of projects, students would have been exposed to a wide variety of projects by the time they leave the elementary grades.

PROJECT LIST

advertisement
award
banner
biography
book
book jacket
bulletin board
cartoon
catalog
charade
chart
choral reading
code
collage
collection
comic book
computer program
contest
conversation
costume
crossword puzzle
dance
demonstration
design
diary
dictionary
diorama
display or exhibit
doll
drawing
dream
dress up as character
epitaph
exhibit

experiment
fable
family tree (geneology)
field trip
film
filmstrip
fingerprint picture
flannel board story
flipbook
food
gameboard and pieces
graph
greeting card
interview
joke
kite
legend
letter
letterhead
life-sized picture
map
mask
menu
mobile
model
mosaic
mural
myth
newspaper
newspaper article
obituary
origami
painting
pantomime

photograph
plaque
play
poem
poster
puppet
puzzle
radio broadcast
readers' theater
rebus
riddle
role play
scavenger hunt
series of pictures
shield
slide show
slogan
song
souvenir
speech
story
survey
symbol
tall tale
time line
tombstone
totem pole
transparency
travel folder
TV quiz show
TV show
video
word search

PROJECT AND PROJECT PLAN EVALUATIONS

Skill Reinforced

Improving research skills

Type of Activity

Paper and pencil

Grade Level: 3+

Time Required

One session minimum

Prerequisite

PROJECT PLAN
PROJECT FILE

Materials

Reproduce appropriate evaluation form in multiple copies:
Evaluation Form for Project Plans (half page form) is for research
Project Evaluation Form (quarter page form) is for book reports

Procedure

1. The teacher, student, or both fill out the evaluation form.
2. Staple the completed forms to project plans for future reference.

Variation

Some items might be deleted from the evaluation form if they are not necessary for the current project. For instance, if the class as a whole determines the research questions to be used, there is no need on the individual evaluation to include a space for research questions. More points could be given for some items, fewer points for others depending on the current emphasis.

Notes: The Evaluation Form for Project Plans is designed to evaluate the research planning process the students are going through, not the end product. That is why completing the project, while a necessary skill, is considered extra credit on this form.
The shorter Project Evaluation Form is good to use in making the Project File notebook because it concentrates on both the product and the process.
Encourage students to keep copies of their own project plans and evaluation forms to aid them in planning future projects.

EVALUATION FORM FOR PROJECT PLANS
(10 points possible for each item)

Name _____   Room number _____

# of Points	Item	Comments (check suitable remarks)	
_____	key word bank	_____ sufficient	_____ insufficient
_____	research questions	_____ appropriate	_____ inappropriate
_____	resource list	_____ variety	_____ try more types
_____	project type	_____ appropriate	_____ try something else
_____	material list	_____ complete	_____ incomplete
_____	list of steps	_____ clear	_____ unclear
_____	time allowed	_____ realistic	_____ unrealistic
_____	rough draft picture	_____ clear	_____ unclear
_____	notes	_____ own words	_____ not sentences
		_____ pictures	
		_____ sufficient	_____ insufficient
_____	bibliography	_____ correct	_____ incorrect
_____	project (extra credit) (overall appearance, title, facts, pictures)		

⬜ TOTAL POINTS

Project Evaluation Form	Project Evaluation Form
Name	Name
Project title or short description	Project title or short description
What did I do well?	What did I do well?
What would I improve next time?	What would I improve next time?

APPENDIX

SKILL RODEO AWARDS

Skill Reinforced

Recognizing students' progress in acquiring library research skills

Type of Activity

Awards

Grade Level: 1–6

Materials

Award forms, reproduced and filled in

Procedure

1. Identify the skills the student must demonstrate to earn each award. Each year a student could earn one award, for example:

   First grade: Best Brander
   Second grade: Trick Rider
   Third grade: Top-notch Roper
   Fourth-Sixth grade: Champion Wrangler

   Or, he could earn all of them over one year depending on how the program is set up.
2. Distribute awards to students at an awards assembly or as students earn them.

Examples of Prerequisites

Best Brander

- identifies specific areas of LMC (LE GRAND TOUR; EGG HUNT)
- identifies author, title, and call number on book (LINE 'EM UP, MOVE 'EM OUT; STEPPIN' TIME)
- knows ABC order (FAIRY TALE CODES; NURSERY RHYME CODES)
- knows where to find index and table of contents in a nonfiction book (MOTHER GOOSE BOOK)
- begins to take notes in own words (THAT'S A FACT)
- begins to record bibliographic data (READING WREATHS)

Trick Rider

- recognizes call numbers and identifies appropriate LMC section (AROUND THE WORLD)
- locates fiction and nonfiction books on shelf using call number (CHOOSE AND CHECK: Fiction and Nonfiction Call Numbers; WHAT'S MY POSITION?)
- uses guide words to locate words in dictionary and correct volume of encyclopedia (GUIDE WORD PUZZLES; FROM WHICH TREE DID I FALL?; WHICH VOLUME?; CHOOSE AND CHECK: Before, After, or On That Page!; CHOOSE AND CHECK: Am I in This Volume?)
- looks up subjects in the card catalog and encyclopedias (CARD CATALOG SEARCH; ENCYCLOPEDIA SEARCH)
- take notes in own words (LET YOUR KNOWLEDGE BLOSSOM)
- records bibliographic data (READING WREATHS; LET YOUR KNOWLEDGE BLOSSOM)
- recognizes LMC vocabulary and meanings (WE'VE GOT RHYTHM)
- looks up information using an index (NURSERY RHYME PUZZLES)

- begins to think of additional key words (BRAINSTORMING)
- begins to visualize research process (CLIMB MOUNT EVEREST)

Top-notch Roper

- picks correct reference book to answer questions (PUT HUMPTY DUMPTY TOGETHER EGGS-ACTLY; WHO'S GOT THE ANSWER)
- identifies information on catalog card (CHOOSE AND CHECK: Catalog Cards)
- takes and organizes notes (LET YOUR KNOWLEDGE BLOSSOM)
- identifies and records bibliographic data (READING WREATHS; FRACTURED BIBLIOGRAPHIES; LET YOUR KNOWLEDGE BLOSSOM)
- recognizes LMC vocabulary and meanings (RIDDLE CHANTS)
- continues to think of key words (BRAINSTORMING; THE UMBRELLA EFFECT)
- plans projects for research (PROJECT PLANS)
- develops map coordinate skills (DESIGN MAGIC)
- visualizes research process (RIBBIT; RESEARCH IMAGERY)

Champion Wrangler

- is adept at using the card catalog, general reference books (for example, encyclopedias and dictionaries), and the LMC (REFERENCE RACE; CONCENTRATION; MEDIA CENTER MAZE)
- can use a periodical index (CHOOSE AND CHECK: Periodical Entries; NATIONAL GEOGRAPHIC INDEX)
- uses map skills (PRESIDENTIAL CITIES IN THE U.S.A.)
- can locate a variety of materials on a specified subject (SCAVENGER HUNT)
- takes notes and organizes information (ANIMAL SAFARI; THE RIGHT WAY)
- plans and carries out a project (PROJECT PLANS)
- remembers to keep a bibliography of resources (READING WREATH, RECORD THAT SOURCE)
- recognizes LMC vocabulary and meanings (WRITING ON THE WALL)
- develops vocabulary using a thesaurus (AN OCEAN OF WORDS)
- is adept at thinking of key words (BRAINSTORMING; THE UMBRELLA EFFECT)
- visualizes the research process (RESEARCH IMAGERY)
- plans and evaluates a variety of projects (PROJECT AND PROJECT PLAN EVALUATIONS)

Skill Rodeo Award

_____

has earned the right to be called

Trick Rider

_____   _____
date   Teacher/Media Specialist

Skill Rodeo Award

_____

has earned the right to be called

Champion Wrangler

_____   _____
date   Teacher/Media Specialist

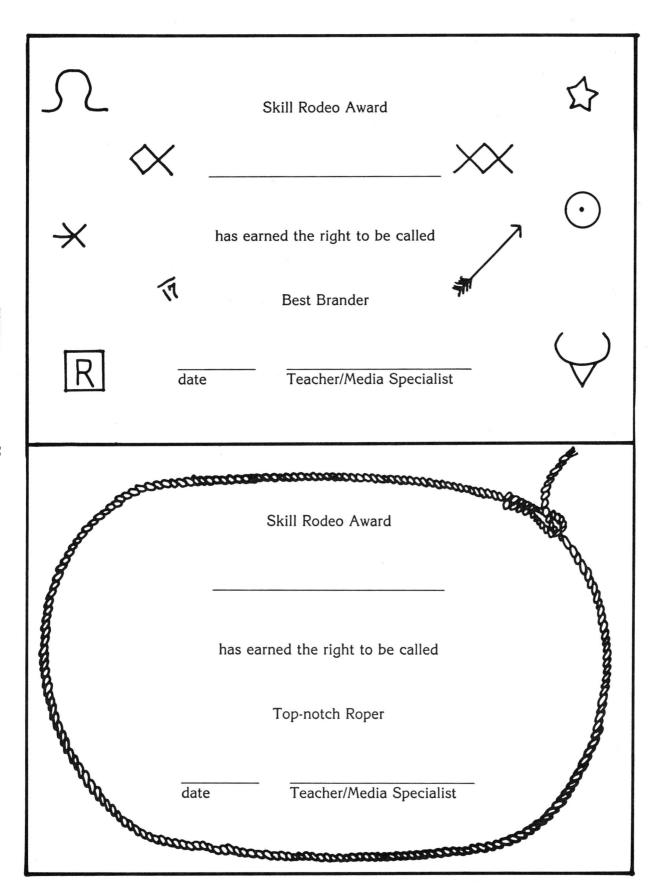

Skill Rodeo Award

_____

has earned the right to be called

Best Brander

_____   _____
date   Teacher/Media Specialist

Skill Rodeo Award

_____

has earned the right to be called

Top-notch Roper

_____   _____
date   Teacher/Media Specialist

TITLE INDEX

TYPE OF ACTIVITY INDEX

Whole Class

*denotes activity that must be done in LMC

Small Group

Partners

Individual

Centers

Art

Drama/Movement

Game

Paper and Pencil